knitted nursery rhymes

knitted nursery rhymes

Recreate the traditional tales with knitted toys

Sarah Keen

First published 2013 by
Guild of Master Craftsman Publications Ltd
Castle Place, 166 High Street, Lewes,
East Sussex BN7 1XU

Text and designs © Sarah Keen, 2013
Copyright in the Work © GMC Publications Ltd, 2013

Technical illustrations by Simon Rodway, except for page 134 (left)
by Sarah Keen.

ISBN 978 1 86108 941 0

Publisher: Jonathan Bailey
Production Manager: Jim Bulley
Managing Editor: Gerrie Purcell
Senior Project Editor: Dominique Page
Editor: Cath Senker
Managing Art Editor: Gilda Pacitti
Designers: Ginny Zeal and Rob Janes
Photographer: Andrew Perris

Set in Frutiger
Colour origination by GMC Reprographics
Printed and bound in China

Dedicated to

Anna

Where you'll find the characters

Introduction

It has been a joy creating the designs for this book, which include many well-known nursery rhymes. Young children will love them because they can play with the toys while learning the words of the rhyme. It is well worth the effort and love that goes into the making of these appealing toys. Every child will have hours of fun and laughter playing games with these gorgeous knitted characters.

I have enjoyed writing these patterns and hope you, too, find pleasure in the projects you decide to make.

Sarah Keen

Jack and Jill

Jack and Jill went up the hill,
To fetch a pail of water;
Jack fell down and broke his crown,
And Jill came tumbling after.

Up Jack got, and home did trot,
As fast as he could caper;
He went to bed to mend his head,
With vinegar and brown paper.

Baa, Baa, Black Sheep

Baa, baa, black sheep,
Have you any wool?
Yes sir, yes sir,
Three bags full:
One for the master,
And one for the dame,
And one for the little boy
Who lives down the lane.

Humpty Dumpty

Humpty Dumpty sat on a wall,
Humpty Dumpty had a great fall;
All the king's horses and all the king's men
Couldn't put Humpty together again.

Mary Had a Little Lamb

Mary had a little lamb,
Its fleece was white as snow,
And everywhere that Mary went,
The lamb was sure to go.

It followed her to school one day,
It was against the rule;
It made the children laugh and play
To see a lamb at school.

And so the teacher turned it out,
But still it lingered near;
And waited patiently about
Till Mary did appear.

'Why does the lamb love Mary so?'
The eager children cry.
'Why Mary loves the lamb, you know,'
The teacher did reply.

Little Boy Blue

Little Boy Blue, come blow your horn,
The sheep's in the meadow, the cow's in the corn;
But where is the little boy who looks after the sheep?
He's under the haystack, fast asleep.

Mary, Mary, Quite Contrary

Mary, Mary, quite contrary,
How does your garden grow?
With silver bells and cockle shells,
And pretty maids all in a row.

Little Miss Muffet

Little Miss Muffet,
Sat on a tuffet,
Eating her curds and whey;
Along came a spider,
Who sat down beside her,
And frightened Miss Muffet away.

Hickory, Dickory, Dock

Hickory, dickory, dock,
The mouse ran up the clock;
The clock struck one,
The mouse ran down,
Hickory, dickory, dock.

Little Bo Peep

Little Bo Peep has lost her sheep,
And doesn't know where to find them;
Leave them alone, and they will come home,
Wagging their tails behind them.

LITTLE BO PEEP >> 94

Hey Diddle Diddle

Hey diddle diddle,
The cat and the fiddle,
The cow jumped over the moon;
The little dog laughed,
To see such fun,
And the dish ran away with the spoon.

HEY DIDDLE DIDDLE >> 98

Five Little Ducks

Five little ducks went swimming one day
Over the hill and far away.
Mother duck said, `Quack, quack, quack, quack',
But only four little ducks came swimming back.

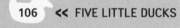

Four little ducks went swimming one day,
Over the hill and far away.
Mother duck said, `Quack, quack, quack, quack',
But only three little ducks came swimming back.

Three little ducks went swimming one day,
Over the hill and far away.
Mother duck said, `Quack, quack, quack, quack',
But only two little ducks came swimming back.

Two little ducks went swimming one day,
Over the hill and far away.
Mother duck said, `Quack, quack, quack, quack',
But only one little duck came swimming back.

One little duck went swimming one day,
Over the hill and far away.
Mother duck said, `Quack, quack, quack, quack',
And all five little ducks came swimming back.

Old Mother Hubbard

Old Mother Hubbard,
went to the cupboard,
To get her poor dog a bone;
But when she got there,
the cupboard was bare,
And so the poor dog had none.

One, Two, Three, Four, Five

One, two, three, four, five,
Once I caught a fish alive;
Six, seven, eight, nine, ten,
Then I let it go again.

Why did you let it go?
Because it bit my finger so.
Which finger did it bite?
This little finger on the right.

Five Little Monkeys

Five little monkeys jumping on the bed,
One fell off and bumped his head.
Mama called the doctor and the doctor said,
`No more monkeys jumping on the bed!'

Four little monkeys jumping on the bed,
One fell off and bumped his head.
Mama called the doctor and the doctor said,
`No more monkeys jumping on the bed!'

Three little monkeys jumping on the bed,
One fell off and bumped his head.
Mama called the doctor and the doctor said,
'No more monkeys jumping on the bed!'

Two little monkeys jumping on the bed,
One fell off and bumped his head.
Mama called the doctor and the doctor said,
'No more monkeys jumping on the bed!'

One little monkey jumping on the bed,
One fell off and bumped his head.
Mama called the doctor and the doctor said,
'Put those monkeys back in bed!'

Girls and Boys Come Out to Play

Girls and boys, come out to play,
The moon doth shine as bright as day;
Leave your supper, and leave your sleep,
And come with your playfellows in the street.

Come with a whoop, come with a call,
Come with a good will or not at all;
Up the ladder and down the wall,
A half-penny roll will serve us all.

The projects

JACK AND JILL

Information you'll need

Finished size
Jack and Jill measure 9in (23cm) high
Bucket measures 2½in (7cm) high

Materials
Any DK (US: light worsted) yarn
Note: amounts are approximate
5g dark blue (A)
20g pale pink (B)
20g grey (C)
25g white (D)
15g blue (E)
15g brown (F)
20g yellow (G)
5g purple (H)
30g rose pink (I)
10g red (J)
5g pale blue (K)
Oddments of black, red and pale
pink for embroidery

1 pair of 3.25mm (UK10:US3) needles and
1 spare needle the same size
Knitters' blunt-ended pins and a needle for
sewing up
Tweezers for stuffing small parts (optional)
Acrylic toy stuffing
Pipe cleaner
Red pencil for shading cheeks

Tension
26 sts x 34 rows to 4in (10cm) square over
st st using 3.25mm needles and DK yarn
before stuffing.

Special abbreviation
M1: Pick up the horizontal loop
between the needles from front to
back and work into the back of it.

How to make Jack
Shoes, Legs, Body and Head
Right shoe and leg
Beg at sole of shoe using the thumb method and A, cast on 14 sts.
Place a marker on cast-on edge between the 5th and 6th st of the sts just cast on.
Row 1 (WS): Purl.
Row 2: K2, (m1, k2) to end (20 sts).
Beg with a p row, work 5 rows in st st.
Shape shoe
Row 8: (K1, k2tog) twice, k2, (k2tog, k1) twice, k6 (16 sts).
Row 9: Purl.
Change to B for leg and dec:
Row 10: (K2, k2tog) twice, k8 (14 sts).
Beg with a p row, work 23 rows in st st.
Break yarn and set aside.
Left shoe and leg
Beg at sole of shoe using the thumb method and A, cast on 14 sts.
Place a marker on cast-on edge between the 9th and 10th st of the sts just cast on.
Row 1 (WS): Purl.
Row 2: K2, (m1, k2) to end (20 sts).
Beg with a p row, work 5 rows in st st.
Shape shoe
Row 8: K7, (k2tog, k1) twice, (k1, k2tog) twice, k1 (16 sts).
Row 9: Purl.
Change to B for leg and dec:
Row 10: K8, (k2tog, k2) twice (14 sts).
Beg with a p row, work 23 rows in st st.
Join legs
Change to C for lower body and k across sts of left leg and then with the same yarn, cont knitting across sts of right leg (28 sts).
Beg with a p row, work 7 rows in st st. **
Change to D for upper body and work 14 rows in st st.

Change to B for head and work 2 rows in st st.
Next row: *K4, (m1, k2) 4 times, k2, rep from * once (36 sts).
Beg with a p row, work 15 rows in st st.
Shape top of head
Next row: (K2tog, k2) to end (27 sts).
Next and foll alt row: Purl.
Next row: (K2tog, k1) to end (18 sts).
Next row: (K2tog) to end (9 sts).
Thread yarn through sts on needle and leave loose.

Sleeves and Hands (make 2)
Beg at shoulder using the thumb method and D for sleeve, cast on 4 sts.
Row 1 (WS): Purl.

Row 2: K1, (m1, k1) to end (7 sts).
Row 3: Purl.
Row 4: K1, m1, k to last st, m1, k1 (9 sts).
Rows 5 to 8: Rep rows 3 and 4, twice (13 sts).
Place a marker on first and last st of last row.
Beg with a p row, work 13 rows in st st.
Row 22: K3, (k2tog, k3) twice (11 sts).
Change to B for hand and beg with a p row, work 5 rows in st st.
Row 28: K2tog, (k1, k2tog) to end (7 sts).
Thread yarn through sts on needle, pull tight and secure by threading yarn a second time through sts.

Cuffs (make 2)
Using the thumb method and D for cuffs,
cast on 15 sts, RS facing to beg.
Cast off p-wise.

Hair
Beg at lower edge using the thumb
method and F, cast on 36 sts and work
in garter st.
Work 22 rows in garter st.

Shape crown
Row 23 (RS): (K2tog, k2) to end (27 sts).
Row 24 and foll alt row: Knit.
Row 25: (K2tog, k1) to end (18 sts).
Row 27: (K2tog) to end (9 sts).
Thread yarn through sts on needle,
pull tight and secure by threading yarn
a second time through sts.

Dungarees
Right leg
Beg at lower edge using the thumb
method and E, cast on 22 sts, RS facing
to beg.
Work 2 rows in garter st.
Beg with a k row, work 22 rows in st st.
Cast off 2 sts at beg of next 2 rows
(18 sts).
Break yarn and set aside.
Left leg
Work as right leg but do not break yarn.
Join legs
With RS facing, k across sts of left leg and
then with the same yarn, cont knitting
across sts of right leg (36 sts).
  Beg with a p row, work 5 rows in st st.
  Work 3 rows in garter st, ending with
  a RS row.
  **Shape back
  Cast off 10 sts k-wise, k15 (16 sts now
on RH needle), cast off 10 sts and fasten
off (16 sts).
Work bib
Rejoin yarn to sts and dec:
Next row: K2tog, k to last 2 sts, k2tog tbl
(14 sts).
Next row: K2, p to last 2 sts, k2.
Next row: K2, k2tog, k to last 4 sts, k2tog
tbl, k2 (12 sts).

Next row: K2, p to last 2 sts, k2.
Next row: Knit.
Rep last 2 rows 3 times more, ending
with a RS row.
Cast off k-wise.

Straps (make 2)
Using the thumb method and E, cast
on 22 sts, RS facing to beg.
K 1 row.
Cast off k-wise.

Straw Hat
Note: Straw hat is knitted throughout
using two strands of G treated as
one strand.
Wind G into two separate balls before beg.
Using the thumb method and G
(2 strands), cast on 49 sts.
Rows 1 and 2: Knit.
Row 3 (RS): K1, (k2tog, k4) to end
(41 sts).
Row 4: Knit.
Row 5: K1, (k2tog, k3) to end (33 sts).
Rows 6 to 11: Purl.
Rows 12 to 14: Knit.
Row 15: K1, (k2tog, k2) to end (25 sts).
Row 16 and foll alt row: Knit.
Row 17: K1, (k2tog, k1) to end (17 sts).
Row 19: K1, (k2tog) to end (9 sts).
Thread yarn through sts on needle,
pull tight and secure by threading yarn
a second time through sts.

Making up

Shoes, Legs, Body and Head

Sew up row ends of shoes and with markers at tips of toes, oversew cast on stitches; leg seam will be ¼in (6mm) on inside edge of heel. Sew up ankles and place a ball of stuffing into toes. Sew up row ends of legs and sew round crotch. Stuff legs and sew up body seam. Stuff body and sew up row ends of head to halfway up head. Stuff head, pulling stitches on a thread tight at top of head and sew up remainder of row ends. To shape neck, take a double length of yarn to match upper body and sew a running stitch round last row of body, sewing in and out of every half stitch. Pull tight and knot yarn, sewing ends into neck.

Sleeves and Hands

Sew up row ends of hands and place a small ball of stuffing into hands, pushing stuffing in with tweezers or tip of scissors. Sew up sleeves from wrists to markers at underarm. Stuff sleeves leaving armholes open. Sew arms to doll at either side, sewing cast-on stitches at top of arms to second row below neck.

Cuffs

Place cuffs around wrists and join row ends. Sew cuffs to wrists using backstitch down centre of cuff, all the way round.

Features

Start and finish off features at top of head under hair. Embroider eyes in black, marking their position on 9th row above neck with three clear knitted stitches in between. Work two vertical stitches close together starting at marked position and ending two knitted rows above the marked position. Repeat for the other eye. Embroider mouth in red on the 4th and 5th rows below eyes, making a shallow 'v' shape across three stitches. Embroider nose in B at centre front on row below eyes, making a bundle of five horizontal stitches over one stitch. Shade cheeks with a red pencil.

Hair

Sew up row ends of hair and place on doll with seam at centre back, pulling hair down to neck at back. Sew lower edge of hair to head using backstitch all the way round.

Dungarees and Straps

Oversew leg seams of dungarees on right side from lower edge to crotch. Sew round crotch and sew up row ends at centre back. Place dungarees on doll and sew cast-off stitches at waist to first row of upper body using backstitch. Sew ends of straps to bib, take straps over shoulders, cross them over and sew ends to waist of dungarees at back.

Straw Hat

Sew up row ends of straw hat and place on head. Sew inside edge of brim to head all the way round, using backstitch on right side, sewing through brim to head.

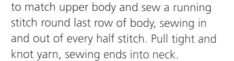

How to make Jill
Shoes, Legs, Body and Head
Make Shoes, Legs, Body and Head as Jack using H for shoes, D for lower body and I for upper body.

Sleeves, Arms and Hands (make 2)
Beg at shoulder using the thumb method and I for sleeve cast on 4 sts.
Row 1 (WS): Purl.
Row 2: K1, (m1, k1) to end (7 sts).
Row 3: Purl.
Row 4: K1, m1, k to last st, m1, k1 (9 sts).
Rows 5 to 8: Rep rows 3 and 4 twice (13 sts).
Place a marker on first and last st of last row.
P 2 rows then k 1 row.
Change to B for arm and beg with a k row, work 10 rows in st st.
Row 22: K3, (k2tog, k3) twice (11 sts).
Place a marker on last row for wrist gathering.
Beg with a p row, work 5 rows in st st.
Row 28: K2tog, (k1, k2tog) to end (7 sts).
Thread yarn through sts on needle, pull tight and secure by threading yarn a second time through sts.

Skirt of Dress and Apron Bib
Beg at lower edge of skirt of dress using the thumb method and I, cast on 54 sts and beg in garter st.
Work 2 rows in garter st.
Beg with a k row, work 16 rows in st st.
Row 19 (RS): (K2tog, k4) to end (45 sts).
Beg with a p row, work 5 rows in st st.
Change to D for waistband of apron and dec:
Row 25: (K2tog, k3) to end (36 sts).
Work 2 rows in garter st, ending with a RS row.

Shape back
Cont in D and shape back and work bib as dungarees for Jack from ** to end.

Apron
Beg at lower edge using the thumb method and D, cast on 14 sts and beg in garter st.
Work 2 rows in garter st.
Row 3 (RS): Knit.
Row 4: K2, p10, k2.
Rows 5 to 18: Rep rows 3 and 4, 7 times more.
Cast off k-wise.

Neck Strap
Using the thumb method and D, cast on 30 sts, RS facing to beg.
Row 1: Knit.
Cast off k-wise.

Bow
Using the thumb method and D, cast on 35 sts, RS facing to beg.
Cast off p-wise.

Hair
Make Hair as Jack using F.

Headscarf
Using the thumb method and D, cast on 56 sts and work in patt.
Join on J and work in D and J, carrying yarn loosely up side of work.
Row 1 (RS): Using J, k2, (s1p, k2) to end.
Row 2: Using J, p2, (s1p, p2) to end.
Row 3: Using D, knit.
Row 4: Using D, knit.
Rows 5 to 8: Rep rows 1 to 4 once.
Row 9: Using J, K2tog, (s1p, k2) to last 3 sts, s1p, k2tog tbl (54 sts).
Row 10: Using J, p1, (s1p, p2) to last 2 sts, s1p, p1.
Row 11: Using D, k2tog, k to last 2 sts, k2tog tbl (52 sts).
Row 12: Using D, k2tog, k to last 2 sts, k2tog tbl (50 sts).
Rows 13 to 44: Rep rows 9 to 12, 8 times more (2 sts).
Row 45: Using D, k2tog tbl (1 st).
Fasten off.

Making up

Shoes, Legs, Body and Head

Make up Shoes, Legs, Body and Head
as Jack.

Sleeves, Arms and Hands

Sew up row ends of hands and place a
small ball of stuffing into hands, pushing
stuffing in with tweezers or tip of scissors.
Sew up arms from wrists to markers at
underarm. Stuff sleeves leaving armholes
open. To shape wrists, take a double length
of yarn B and sew a running stitch around
row with marker on at wrist, sewing in and
out of every half stitch. Pull tight and knot
yarn, sewing ends into wrist. Sew arms to
doll at either side, sewing cast-on stitches
at top of arms to second row below neck.

Skirt of Dress and Neck Strap

Sew up row ends of skirt of dress and with
seam at centre back, place skirt of dress on
doll. Sew cast-off stitches at waist to first
row of upper body. Sew one end of neck
strap to bib, take strap around neck and
sew the other end to the other side of bib.

Apron

Sew cast-off stitches of apron to waistband
on doll at centre front. Sew lower edge of
apron to skirt.

Bow

Shape bow into a bow shape and sew
to waistband of apron at back.

Features

Embroider Features as Jack.

Hair

Make up Hair as Jack.

Headscarf

Place headscarf around head and join
at back. Sew lower edge in place around
head and fold point of headscarf down
at back and sew in place.

How to make Bucket

Bucket

Using the thumb method and C, cast on 32 sts.

Work 2 rows in garter st.

Beg with a k row, work 2 rows in st st.

Row 5 (RS): (K5, k2tog, k2, k2tog, k5) twice (28 sts).

Beg with a p row, work 5 rows in st st.

Row 11: (K4, k2tog, k2, k2tog, k4) twice (24 sts).

Beg with a p row, work 3 rows in st st.

Rows 15 and 16: P 2 rows for fold line.

Row 17: (K2tog, k1) to end (16 sts).

Row 18: Purl.

Row 19: (K2tog) to end (8 sts).

Thread yarn though sts on needle, pull tight and secure by threading yarn a second time through sts.

Water

Using the thumb method and K, cast on 28 sts.

Row 1 (WS): Purl.

Row 2: (K2tog, k2) to end (21 sts).

Row 3: (P1, p2tog) to end (14 sts).

Row 4: (K2tog) to end (7 sts).

Thread yarn through sts on needle, pull tight and secure by threading yarn a second time through sts.

Handle

Using the thumb method and C, cast on 18 sts, WS facing to beg.

Beg with a p row, work 4 rows in st st, ending with a k row.

Cast off p-wise.

Making up

Bucket

Sew up row ends of bucket and stuff.

Water

Sew up row ends of water and sew outside edge of water to inside rim of bucket.

Handle

Take the pipe cleaner and fold in half and cut to length of handle. Join cast-on and cast-off stitches of handle, enclosing pipe cleaner inside. Curve handle and sew ends to top of bucket.

BAA, BAA, BLACK SHEEP

Information you'll need

Finished size
Master measures 9in (23cm) high
Dame measures 9in (23cm) high
Sheep measures 4½in (11.5cm) high
Sacks of Wool measure 3in (8cm) high
Little Boy measures 6½in (16.5cm) high

Materials
Any DK (US: light worsted) yarn
Note: Amounts are approximate
10g air force blue (A)
10g silver grey (B)
5g white (C)
10g mustard (D)
15g pale pink (E)
10g red (F)
35g black (G)
10g brown (H)
5g dark green (I)
5g dark brown (J)
5g claret (K)
15g raspberry pink (L)
5g cream (M)
10g fawn (N)
5g purple (O)
5g green (P)
5g pale brown (Q)
5g blue (R)
5g grey (S)
10g dark grey (T)
15g oatmeal (U)
Oddments of black, red, pale pink and grey
for embroidery
1 pair of 3.25mm (UK10:US3) needles
and a spare needle the same size
Knitters' blunt-ended pins and a needle
for sewing up
Tweezers for stuffing small parts (optional)
Pencil for loop stitch
Acrylic toy stuffing
Plastic drinking straw
Pipe cleaner
Red pencil for shading cheeks

Tension
26 sts x 34 rows to 4in (10cm) square over
st st using 3.25mm needles and DK yarn
before stuffing.

Special abbreviation
M1: Pick up the horizontal loop between
the needles from front to back and work
into the back of it.

How to make Master

Shoes, Legs, Body and Head

Make Shoes, Legs, Body and Head as Jack on page 34, using A for shoes, B for legs, C for lower body and D for upper body.

Breeches and Belt

Right leg

Beg at lower edge using the thumb method and F, cast on 20 sts.
P 1 row then k 1 row.
Row 3 (RS): K9, m1, k2, m1, k9 (22 sts).
Beg with a p row, work 13 rows in st st.
Cast off 2 sts at beg of next 2 rows (18 sts).
Break yarn and set aside.

Left leg

Work as right leg but do not break yarn.

Join legs

With RS facing, k across sts of left leg and then with the same yarn, cont knitting across sts of right leg (36 sts).
Beg with a p row, work 5 rows in st st.
Change to G for belt and work 3 rows in garter st, ending with a RS row.
Cast off in garter st.

Sleeves and Hands (make 2)

Make Sleeves and Hands as Jack on page 34, using D for sleeve.

Cuffs (make 2)

Make Cuffs as Jack on page 35, using D.

Hair

Make Hair as Jack on page 35, using H.

Waistcoat

Beg at lower edge using the thumb method and A, cast on 36 sts and work in garter st, RS facing to beg.
Work 13 rows in garter st, ending with a RS row.
Divide for fronts and back.
Row 14: K5, cast off next 4 sts (6 sts now on RH needle) k17, cast off next 4 sts, k4 (28 sts).
Next row: K5, turn and work on these 5 sts.
Work 16 rows in garter st, ending with a RS row.
Cast off in garter st and fasten off.
Rejoin yarn to rem sts.
Next row: K18, turn and work on these 18 sts.
Work 16 rows in garter st, ending with a RS row.
Cast off in garter st and fasten off.
Rejoin yarn to rem sts and work 17 rows in garter st, ending with a RS row.
Cast off in garter st.

Hat

Beg at brim using the thumb method and F, cast on 55 sts and beg in garter st.
Work 4 rows in garter st.
Change to D and dec.
Row 5 (RS): (K2tog, k3) to end (44 sts).
P 1 row then k 1 row.
Rejoin F and cont in F and beg with a p row, work 3 rows in st st.
Row 11: (K2tog, k18, k2tog tbl) twice (40 sts).
Row 12 and foll 2 alt rows: Purl.
Row 13: (K2tog, k16, k2tog tbl) twice (36 sts).
Row 15: (K2tog, k14, k2tog tbl) twice (32 sts).
Row 17: (K2tog) twice, k8, k2tog, k2tog tbl, (k2tog) twice, k8, k2tog, k2tog tbl (24 sts).
Cast off p-wise.

Feather

Using the thumb method and I, cast on 8 sts.

Row 1 (WS): Purl.
Row 2: K5, turn.
Row 3: S1p, p to end.
Row 4: Knit.
Cast off p-wise.

Bow

Using the thumb method and I, cast on 5 sts and work in garter st, RS facing to beg. Work 5 rows in garter st.
Cast off in garter st.

Stick

Using the thumb method and J, cast on 5 sts and work in rev st st, RS facing to beg. Beg with a p row, rev st st for 6in (15cm).
Cast off.

Making up

Shoes, Legs, Body and Head

Make up Shoes, Legs, Body and Head as Jack on page 36.

Breeches and Belt

Sew up all seams on right side and sew up row ends of each leg from lower edge to crotch. Sew round crotch and sew up row ends at centre back. Sew up row ends of belt and place breeches on doll. Sew belt to first row of upper body using backstitch all the way round.

Sleeves and Hands

Make up Sleeves and Hands as Jack on page 36.

Cuffs

Make up Cuffs as Jack on page 36.

Features

Embroider features as Jack on page 36. Embroider buckle in grey taking a horizontal stitch above and below belt and join these with a double stitch at each side to form a rectangle (see page 139 for how to begin and fasten off the embroidery invisibly).

Hair

Make up Hair as Jack on page 36.

Waistcoat

Sew up shoulder seams of waistcoat and place on doll. Sew cast-off stitches at neck to back of neck.

Hat

Fold cast-off stitches of hat in half and sew up. Sew up row ends of hat and lightly stuff top of hat and place on head. Sew in place using backstitch at base of brim, sewing through hat to head.

Feather

Fold feather lengthwise and sew up cast-on and cast-off stitches along feather. Sew feather to side of hat.

Bow

To shape bow, wind matching yarn around middle of bow a few times and tie ends at back. Sew bow to centre front of neck.

Stick

Cut drinking straw to 5in (13cm). Fold a 6in (15cm) length of pipe cleaner in half and in half again. Push folded pipe cleaner into top of straw with ½in (1.5cm) of pipe cleaner showing at top. Sew up row ends of stick around straw and gather round stitches at top and bottom and pull tight and secure. Bend top of stick over slightly and sew stick to hand of doll.

baa, baa, black sheep

How to make Dame

Slippers, Legs, Body and Head

Right slipper and leg

Beg at sole of slipper using the thumb method and K, cast on 14 sts.

Place a marker on cast-on edge between the 5th and 6th st of the sts just cast on.

Row 1 (WS): Purl.

Row 2: K2, (m1, k2) to end (20 sts).

Beg with a p row, work 3 rows in st st.

Change to E for leg and work 2 rows in st st.

Shape foot

Row 8: (K1, k2tog) twice, k2, (k2tog, k1) twice, k6 (16 sts).

Row 9: Purl.

Row 10: (K2, k2tog) twice, k8 (14 sts).

Beg with a p row, work 23 rows in st st.

Break yarn and set aside.

Left slipper and leg

Beg at sole of slipper using the thumb method and K, cast on 14 sts.

Place a marker on cast-on edge between the 9th and 10th st of the sts just cast on.

Row 1 (WS): Purl.

Row 2: K2, (m1, k2) to end (20 sts).

Beg with a p row, work 3 rows in st st.

Change to E for leg and work 2 rows in st st.

Shape foot

Row 8: K7, (k2tog, k1) twice, (k1, k2tog) twice, k1 (16 sts).

Row 9: Purl.

Row 10: K8, (k2tog, k2) twice, (14 sts).

Beg with a p row, work 23 rows in st st.

Join legs

Change to C for lower body and k across sts of left leg and then with the same yarn, cont knitting across sts of right leg (28 sts).

Beg with a p row, work 9 rows in st st.

Change to L for upper body and work 8 rows in st st.

** Change to E for neck and work 4 rows in st st.

Place a marker on last row for neck gathering.

Work 2 rows in st st.

Next row: *K4, (m1, k2) 4 times, k2, rep from * once (36 sts).

Beg with a p row, work 15 rows in st st.

Shape top of head

Next row: (K2tog, k2) to end (27 sts).

Next and foll alt row: Purl.

Next row: (K2tog, k1) to end (18 sts).

Next row: (K2tog) to end (9 sts).

Thread yarn through sts on needle and leave loose.

Skirt of Dress

Beg at lower edge using the thumb method and L, cast on 80 sts.

Row 1 (WS): Purl.

Row 2: Knit.

Row 3: P1, (p3tog, p2) to last 4 sts, p3tog, p1 (48 sts).

Beg with a k row, work 16 rows in st st.

Row 20: (K6, k2tog, k8, k2tog, k6) twice (44 sts).

Beg with a p row, work 5 rows in st st.

Row 26: (K5, k2tog, k8, k2tog, k5) twice (40 sts).

Beg with a p row, work 5 rows in st st.

Row 32: (K4, k2tog, k8, k2tog, k4) twice (36 sts).

Cast off k-wise.

Sleeves, Arms and Hands (make 2)

Beg at shoulder using the thumb method and L for sleeve, cast on 4 sts.

Row 1 (WS): Purl.

Row 2: K1 (m1, k1) to end (7 sts).

Row 3: Purl.
Row 4: K1, m1, k to last st, m1, k1 (9 sts).
Rows 5 to 8: Rep rows 3 and 4 twice (13 sts).
Place a marker on first and last st of last row.
Row 9: Purl.
Change to E for arm and beg with a k row, work 12 rows in st st.
Row 22: K3, (k2tog, k3) twice (11 sts).
Place a marker on last row for wrist gathering.
Beg with a p row, work 5 rows in st st.
Row 28: K2tog, (k1, k2tog) to end (7 sts).
Thread yarn through sts on needle, pull tight and secure by threading yarn a second time through sts.

Sleeve Frills (make 2)

Using the thumb method and L, cast on 32 sts.
Row 1 (WS): P2, (p3tog, p2) to end (20 sts).
Cast off p-wise.

Neck Band

Using the thumb method and L, cast on 36 sts, RS facing to beg.
Cast off p-wise.

Hair

Make Hair as Jack on page 35, using N.

Beads

Using the thumb method and M, cast on 41 sts.
Row 1 (WS): K1, (yf, k2tog) to end.
Row 2: Knit.
Cast off p-wise.

Bun

Using the thumb method and N, cast on 12 sts and work in garter st.
Work 2 rows in garter st.
Row 3 (RS): (Kfb, k1) to end (18 sts).
Work 5 rows in garter st.
Row 9: (K2tog, k1) to end (12 sts).
Row 10: (K2tog) to end (6 sts).
Thread yarn through sts on needle, pull tight and secure by threading yarn a second time through sts.

Hair Loops (make 4)

Using the thumb method and N, cast on 16 sts, RS facing to beg.
Cast off loosely, p-wise.

Hair Flowers (make 6)

Using the thumb method and O, cast on 9 sts, WS facing to beg.
Thread yarn through sts on needle, pull tight and secure by threading yarn a second time through sts.

baa, baa, black sheep

Making up

Slippers, Legs, Body and Head

Sew up row ends of slippers and with markers at tips of toes, oversew cast-on stitches; leg seam will be ¼in (6mm) on inside edge of heel. Sew up ankles and place a ball of stuffing into toes. Sew up row ends of legs and sew round crotch. Stuff legs and sew up body seam. Stuff body and sew up row ends of head to halfway up head. Stuff head, pulling stitches on a thread tight at top of head and sew up remainder of row ends. To shape neck, take a double length of E and sew a running stitch round row with marker at neck, sewing in and out of every half stitch. Pull tight and knot yarn, sewing ends into neck.

Skirt of Dress

Sew up row ends of skirt of dress and place on doll. Sew cast-off stitches of skirt of dress to first row of upper body all the way round.

Sleeves, Arms and Hands

Sew up row ends of hands and place a small ball of stuffing into hands, pushing stuffing in with tweezers or tip of scissors. Sew up sleeves from fingers to markers at underarm. Stuff sleeves, leaving armholes open. To shape wrists, take a double length of E and sew a running stitch around row with marker on at wrist, sewing in and out of every half stitch. Pull tight and knot yarn, sewing ends into wrist.

Sleeve frills

Place sleeve frills around arms and sew up row ends. Sew cast-off stitches of sleeve frills to first row of sleeve all the way round. Sew arms to doll at either side, sewing cast-on stitches at top of arms to second row below neck.

Neck Band

Place neck band around neck and sew up row ends. Pin and sew neck band around top of dress and over shoulders, using backstitch down centre of band.

Features

Embroider Features as Jack on page 36.

Hair

Make up Hair as Jack on page 36.

Beads

Join cast-on and cast-off stitches of beads by oversewing along the length. Place beads around neck and join row ends. Sew beads to back of neck and to chest all the way round.

Bun

Sew up row ends of bun and stuff, pushing stuffing in with tweezers or tip of scissors. Sew lower edge of bun to top of head all the way round.

Hair Loops and Flowers

Sew up row ends of each hair loop and then sew two hair loops to each side of hair. Sew three flowers together and repeat for remaining three. Sew flowers to top of hair loops at each side.

How to make Black Sheep

Body

Beg at lower edge using the thumb method and G, cast on 32 sts and work in garter st.

Work 2 rows in garter st.

Row 3 (RS): *(K1, m1) twice, k12, (m1, k1) twice, rep from * once (40 sts).

Row 4: Knit.

Row 5: (K1, m1, k18, m1, k1) twice (44 sts).

Work 21 rows in garter st.

Row 27: K2tog, k18, (k2tog) twice, k18, k2tog tbl (40 sts).

Work 3 rows in garter st.

Row 31: (K2tog) twice, k12, (k2tog) 4 times, k12, k2tog, k2tog tbl (32 sts).

Cast off in garter st.

Legs (make 4)

Beg at top edge using the thumb method and T, cast on 13 sts.

Row 1 (WS): P9, turn.

Row 2: S1k, k4, turn.

Row 3: S1p, p to end.

Work 6 rows in st st.

Row 10: K1, (k2tog, k1) to end (9 sts).

Cast off p-wise.

Head

Beg at top edge using the thumb method and G for top of head, cast on 10 sts and beg in garter st.

Row 1 (RS): (Kfb) to end (20 sts).

Work 5 rows in garter st.

Row 7: K3, (k2tog) twice, k6, (k2tog) twice, k3 (16 sts).

Row 8: Knit.

Change to T for face and cont in st st.

Row 9: (K1 tbl) to end.

Row 10 and foll alt row: Purl.

Row 11: K4, m1, k1, m1, k6, m1, k1, m1, k4 (20 sts).

Row 13: K5, m1, k1, m1, k8, m1, k1, m1, k5 (24 sts).

Beg with a p row, work 7 rows in st st.

Row 21: (K2tog, k1) to end (16 sts).

Row 22: Purl.

Row 23: (K2tog) to end (8 sts).

Thread yarn through sts on needle, pull tight and secure by threading yarn a second time through sts.

Ears (make 2)

Using the thumb method and G, cast on 10 sts.

Row 1 (RS): K2, (k3tog) twice, k2 (6 sts).

Cast off k-wise.

Tail

Using the thumb method and G, cast on 6 sts and work in garter st.

Work 4 rows in garter st.

Row 5 (RS): (K2tog) twice, (kfb) twice (6 sts).

Work 5 rows in garter st.

Row 11: (Kfb) twice, (k2tog) twice (6 sts).

Work 5 rows in garter st.

Thread yarn through sts on needle, pull tight and secure by threading yarn a second time through sts.

Making up

Body

Fold cast-on stitches of body in half and sew up. Fold cast-off stitches in half and sew up. Sew up row ends leaving a gap, stuff body and sew up gap.

Legs

Fold cast-off stitches of legs in half and sew up. Sew up row ends of legs and stuff legs and sew to body.

Head

Sew up row ends of head and stuff head and with this seam at centre back, sew up top edge. Pin and sew head to body.

Ears

Fold cast-off stitches of ears in half and sew up. Fold row ends in half and catch in place. Sew ears to head at each side.

Tail

Sew up row ends of tail and sew one end of tail to body.

Features

Mark position of eyes on 5th row below top of face with three clear knitted stitches in between. Embroider eyes in black and work a vertical chain stitch for each eye starting at marked position and ending one knitted row above the marked position. Using picture as a guide, embroider nose and mouth in black using straight stitches (see page 139 for how to begin and fasten off the embroidery invisibly).

How to make
Three Bags of Wool

Sides of bags (make 2 pieces per bag)

Beg at top edge using the thumb method and U, cast on 14 sts, RS of roll top facing to beg.

Beg with a p row, work 5 rows in st st.

Work 2 rows in garter st.

Beg with a k row, work 16 rows in st st.

Place a marker on first and last st of last row.

Work 10 rows in st st.

Cast off.

Wool (make 1 piece per bag)

Using the thumb method and G, cast on 5 sts loosely.

Row 1 (RS): K1, *knit next st leaving it on the needle, bring yarn to front of work between needles and wrap yarn round a pencil to make a loop, take yarn to back of work between needles and k the same st again, slipping st off LH needle, pass the first of these 2 sts over the second and off the needle. (This will now be referred to as loop-st), k1, rep from * once.

Row 2: K1, (kfb, k1) twice (7 sts).

Row 3: K1, (loop-st, k1) to end.

Row 4: Knit.

Row 5: K2, (loop-st, k1) twice, k1.

Row 6: Knit.

Rows 7 to 10: Rep rows 3 to 6.

Row 11: As row 3.

Row 12: K2tog, k to last 2 sts, k2tog tbl (5 sts).

Row 13: K1, (loop-st, k1) twice.

Cast off.

Making up
Bag

Place right sides of two side pieces of bag together matching all edges and sew up row ends from top edge to markers. Sew up cast-off stitches at lower edge. Fold gusset flat by bringing markers and middle of row ends at lower edge together and sew up row ends across sides. Turn right side out. Allow top edge to roll down and join cast-on stitches to garter-stitch row. Stuff bag.

Wool

Sew outer edge of wool to inside edge of rim leaving a gap. Adjust stuffing, adding more, and sew up gap.

How to make Little Boy

Doll

Make Body and Head, Shoes, Socks and Legs as Girls and Boys on page 130, using C for lower body, P for upper body, I for shoes, C for socks.

Sleeves and Hands (make 2)

Beg at shoulder using the thumb method and P, cast on 4 sts.

Row 1 (WS): Purl.

Row 2: K1, m1, k to last st, m1, k1 (6 sts).

Rep first 2 rows twice more (10 sts).

Place a marker on first and last st of last row.

Beg with a p row, work 9 rows in st st.

Row 16: K2, (k2tog, k2) twice (8 sts).

Change to E for hand and beg with a p row, work 4 rows in st st, ending on a k row.

Thread yarn through sts on needle, pull tight and secure by threading yarn a second time through sts.

Cuffs (make 2)

Using the thumb method and P, cast on 12 sts, RS facing to beg.

Cast off p-wise.

Hair

Make Hair as Girls and Boys on page 130, using Q.

Dungarees and Straps

Make Dungarees and Straps as Girls and Boys on pages 130–1, using R.

Cap

Using the thumb method and S, cast on 32 sts.

Row 1 (RS): Knit.

Row 2: Purl.

Row 3: K2, (m1, k4) to last 2 sts, m1, k2 (40 sts).

Beg with a p row, work 3 rows in st st.

Row 7: (K2tog, k3) to end (32 sts).

Row 8 and foll 2 alt rows: Purl.

Row 9: (K2tog, k2) to end (24 sts).

Row 11: (K2tog, k1) to end (16 sts).

Row 13: (K2tog) to end (8 sts).

Thread yarn through sts on needle, pull tight and secure by threading yarn a second time through sts.

Peak

Using the thumb method and S, cast on 8 sts.

Row 1 (WS): Purl.

Row 2: K2, m1, k4, m1, k2 (10 sts).

Beg with a p row, work 3 rows in st st.

Row 6: K2, (k2tog, k2) twice (8 sts).

Cast off p-wise.

Making up

Body and Head, Shoes and Legs

Make up Body and Head, Shoes, Socks and Legs, as Girls and Boys on page 131.

Sleeves and Hands

Sew up row ends of hands and place a small ball of stuffing into hands, pushing stuffing in with tweezers or tip of scissors. Sew up sleeves from wrists to markers at underarm. Stuff arms leaving armholes open. Sew arms to doll at either side, sewing cast-on stitches at top of arms to second row below neck.

Cuffs

Place cuffs around wrists and sew up row ends. Sew cuffs to wrists using backstitch down centre of cuff, all the way round.

Features

Embroider Features as Girls and Boys on page 131.

Hair

Make up Hair as Girls and Boys on page 131.

Dungarees and Straps

Make up Dungarees and Straps as Girls and Boys on pages 130–1.

Cap and Peak

Sew up row ends of cap and stuff lightly around inside corners of hat with no stuffing at crown. Place cap on head and pin and sew lower edge of cap to head, all the way round. With right side of stocking stitch outside, fold peak, bringing cast-on and cast-off stitches together, and sew up these stitches. Gather round row ends of peak, pull tight and secure. Sew peak to lower edge of cap at centre front.

baa, baa, black sheep

HUMPTY DUMPTY

Information you'll need

Finished size
Humpty measures 8in (20cm) high
Wall measures 4in (10cm) high
Soldiers measure 8in (20cm) high
Horses measure 5in (13cm) high

Materials
Any DK (US: light worsted) yarn
Note: Amounts are approximate
25g blue (A)
10g green (B)
20g white (C)
10g buttermilk (D)
25g red (E)
30g brown (F)
25g ginger (G)
10g black (H)
10g pale pink (I)
20g pale brown (J)
10g dark brown (K)
Oddments of black, dark brown,
red, white and gold for embroidery

1 pair of 3.25mm (US3:UK10) needles and
a spare needle of the same size
Knitters' blunt-ended pins and a needle for
sewing up
Tweezers for stuffing small parts (optional)
Acrylic toy stuffing
Thick cardboard (optional)
Red pencil for shading cheeks

Tension
26 sts x 34 rows to 4in (10cm) square over
st st using 3.25mm needles and DK yarn
before stuffing.

Special abbreviation
M1: Pick up the horizontal loop between
the needles from front to back and work
into the back of it.

Legs (make 2)

Using the thumb method and A, cast on 19 sts.

Row 1 and foll 2 alt rows: Purl.

Row 2 (RS): K2tog, k7, m1, k1, m1, k9 (20 sts).

Row 4: K2tog, k7, m1, k1, m1, k10 (21 sts).

Row 6: K2tog, k7, m1, k1, m1, k11 (22 sts).

Beg with a p row, work 3 rows in st st.

Row 10: K1, m1, k6, k2tog tbl, k1, k2tog, k10 (21 sts).

Row 11 and foll alt row: Purl.

Row 12: K1, m1, k6, k2tog tbl, k1, k2tog, k9 (20 sts).

Row 14: K1, m1, k6, k2tog tbl, k1, k2tog, k8 (19 sts).

Row 15: Purl.

Cast off loosely.

Boots (make 2)

Using the thumb method and E, cast on 8 sts.

Row 1 and foll alt row: Purl.

Row 2 (RS): (K1, m1, k2, m1, k1) twice (12 sts).

Row 4: (K1, m1, k1, m1, k2, m1, k1, m1, k1) twice (20 sts).

Beg with a p row, work 3 rows in st st.

Row 8: K8, (k2tog) twice, k8 (18 sts).

Row 9: Purl.

Row 10: K7, (k2tog) twice, k7 (16 sts).

Row 11: P6, (p2tog) twice, p6 (14 sts).

Row 12: K5, (k2tog) twice, k5 (12 sts).

Cast off p-wise.

How to make Humpty Dumpty

Main Piece

Beg at lower edge using the thumb method and A, cast on 11 sts.

Row 1 (WS): Purl.

Row 2: K1, (m1, k1) to end (21 sts). Join on B and work in st st in stripe, carrying yarn loosely up side of work and shape.

Row 3: Using B, purl.

Row 4: Using B, k1, (m1, k2) to end (31 sts).

Row 5: Using A, purl.

Row 6: Using A, k1, (m1, k3) to end (41 sts).

Row 7: Using B, purl.

Row 8: Using B, k1, (m1, k4) to end (51 sts).

Row 9: Using A, purl.

Row 10: Using A, k1, (m1, k5) to end (61 sts).

Rows 11 and 12: Using B, p 1 row then k 1 row.

Rows 13 and 14: Using A, p 1 row then k 1 row.

Rows 15 to 22: Rep rows 11 to 14 twice.

Rows 23 and 24: Using B, p 1 row then k 1 row.

Change to C and beg with a p row, work 3 rows in st st.

Row 28: Purl.

Change to D and beg with a p row, work 11 rows in st st.

Row 40: K1, (k2tog, k8) to end (55 sts).

Row 41 and foll 6 alt rows: Purl.

Row 42: K1, (k2tog, k7) to end (49 sts).

Row 44: K1, (k2tog, k6) to end (43 sts).

Row 46: K1, (k2tog, k5) to end (37 sts).

Row 48: K1, (k2tog, k4) to end (31 sts).

Row 50: K1, (k2tog, k3) to end (25 sts).

Row 52: K1, (k2tog, k2) to end (19 sts).

Row 54: K1, (k2tog, k1) to end (13 sts).

Row 55: P1, (p2tog) to end (7 sts).

Thread yarn through sts on needle, pull tight and secure by threading yarn a second time through sts.

Boot Tops (make 2)

Using the thumb method and E, cast on 24 sts.

Row 1 (RS): K2tog, k to last 2 sts, k2tog tbl (22 sts).

Row 2: P2tog tbl, p to last 2 sts, p2tog (20 sts).

Rows 3 and 4: Rep rows 1 and 2 once (16 sts).

Cast off.

Arms and Gloved Hands (make 2)

Using the thumb method and B, cast on 13 sts.

Beg with a p row, work 9 rows in st st.

Work 2 rows in garter st.

Change to C for gloves.

Row 12 (RS): K1, (k2tog, k1) to end (9 sts)

Row 13 and foll 2 alt rows: Purl.

Row 14: K4, m1, k1, m1, k4 (11 sts).

Row 16: K4, m1, k3, m1, k4 (13 sts).

Row 18: K4, m1, k5, m1, k4 (15 sts).

Row 19: P10, turn.

Row 20: K5.

Break yarn and thread through these 5 sts, pull tight and secure by threading yarn a second time through sts, then join row ends of thumb.

Rejoin yarn to WS of rem sts halfway along row and p to end.

Push rem sts tog and work 2 rows in st st (10 sts).

Row 23: K1, (k2tog, k1) to end (7 sts). Thread yarn though sts on needle, pull tight and secure by threading yarn a second time through sts.

Bow

Using the thumb method and E, cast on 8 sts and work in garter st, RS facing to beg. Work 7 rows in garter st.

Cast off in garter st.

Making up
Main Piece

Gather round cast-on stitches of Humpty Dumpty, pull tight and secure, and sew up row ends, leaving a gap. Stuff and sew up gap.

Legs

Sew up cast-on and cast-off stitches of legs, leaving top and bottom open. Stuff legs through both ends, pushing stuffing in with tweezers or tip of scissors. Position legs and pin and sew to lower edge of main piece.

Boots and Boot Tops

Fold cast-on stitches of boots in half and sew up. Sew up row ends of boots and stuff. Sew boots to lower edge of legs all the way round. Place boot tops around ankles and sew up row ends and sew lower edge of boot tops to boots.

Arms and Gloved Hands

Sew up row ends of hands and stuff hands and thumb, pushing stuffing in with tweezers or tip of scissors. Sew up arms and stuff, pushing stuffing in with tweezers or tip of scissors. Leaving armholes open, sew arms to main piece.

Features

Mark position of eyes on 10th row above collar with clear 5 stitches in between. Embroider eyes in black: make a vertical chain stitch starting at marked position and finish on row above, then work a second chain stitch on top and repeat for other eye (see page 139 for how to begin and fasten off the embroidery invisibly). Work nose in red on row below eyes at centre front, making a bundle of five horizontal stitches over one stitch. Using picture as a guide, embroider mouth in red using backstitch. Shade cheeks with a red pencil.

Bow

To shape bow, wind matching yarn around middle of bow a few times and tie ends at back. Sew bow to centre front of collar.

How to make Wall

Front and Back (make 2 pieces)

Beg at lower edge using the thumb method and F, cast on 53 sts.

Join on G and work in patt, carrying yarn loosely up side of work.

Row 1 (RS): Using G, k5, (s1p, k5) to end.

Row 2: Using G, p5, (s1p, p5) to end.

Rows 3 and 4: Rep rows 1 and 2 once.

Rows 5 and 6: Using F, k 2 rows.

Row 7: Using G, k2, (s1p, k5) to last 3 sts, s1p, k2.

Row 8: Using G, p2, (s1p, p5) to last 3 sts, s1p, p2.

Rows 9 and 10: Rep rows 7 and 8 once.

Rows 11 and 12: Using F, k 2 rows.

Rows 1 to 12 set the patt and are rep twice more, then rows 1 to 5 once. Cast off in F, k-wise.

Sides (make 2)

Using the thumb method and F, cast on 16 sts, WS facing for first row.

Beg with a p row, work 35 rows in st st. Cast off.

Top and Bottom (make 2)

Using the thumb method and F, cast on 16 sts, WS facing for first row.

Beg with a p row, work 69 rows in st st. Cast off.

Making up

Wall, Sides, Top and Bottom

Sew side pieces to sides of front and back wall. Sew top piece to top and stuff. If desired, thick cardboard can be cut to size of front and back and inserted. Sew bottom of wall to complete.

How to make Soldier

Body and Head

Make Body and Head as Girls and Boys on page 130, using C for lower body and E for upper body.

Boots and Legs (make 2)

Beg at sole of boot using the thumb method and H, cast on 10 sts.

Row 1 (WS): Purl.

Row 2: K2, (m1, k2) to end (14 sts).

Beg with a p row, work 3 rows in st st.

Shape boot

Row 6: K5, (k2tog) twice, k5 (12 sts).

Row 7: P3, p2tog, p2, p2tog, p3 (10 sts).

Work 4 rows in st st.

Change to I for leg and work 12 rows in st st.

Cast off.

Trousers

First leg

Beg at lower edge using the thumb method and A, cast on 16 sts, WS facing to beg.

Beg with a p row, work 17 rows in st st.

Cast off 1 st at beg of next 2 rows (14 sts).

Break yarn and set aside.

Second leg

Work as first leg but do not break yarn.

Join legs

With RS facing, k across sts of second leg and then with the same yarn, cont knitting across sts of first leg (28 sts).

Beg with a p row, work 5 rows in st st.

Cast off.

Skirt of Jacket and Belt

Begin at lower edge using the thumb method and E, cast on 33 sts and beg in garter st.

Work 2 rows in garter st.

Beg with a k row, work 4 rows in st st.

Change to C for belt and dec:

Row 7 (RS): K5, (k2tog, k5) to end (29 sts).

Cast off k-wise.

Sleeves and Hands (make 2)

Beg at shoulder using the thumb method and E, cast on 10 sts.

Beg with a p row, work 15 rows in st st.

Row 16 (RS): K2, (k2tog, k2) twice (8 sts).

Change to I for hand and beg with a p row, work 4 rows in st st, ending on a k row.

Thread yarn through sts on needle, pull tight and secure by threading yarn a second time through sts.

Hair

Make Hair as Girls and Boys on page 130, using F.

Hat

Begin at lower edge using the thumb method and H, cast on 26 sts and work in garter st.

Work 4 rows in garter st.

Row 5 (RS): (K4, kfb, k3, kfb, k4) twice (30 sts).

Work 13 rows in garter st.

Row 19: (K2tog, k1) to end (20 sts).

Row 20 and foll alt row: Knit.

Row 21: (K2tog) to end (10 sts).

Row 23: (K2tog) to end (5 sts).

Thread yarn through sts on needle, pull tight and secure by threading yarn a second time through sts.

Making up

Body and Head

Make up Body and Head as Girls and Boys on page 131.

Boots and Legs

Fold cast-on stitches of boots in half and oversew. Sew up row ends of boots and place a ball of stuffing into toes, pushing stuffing in with tweezers or tip of scissors. Sew up row ends of legs and stuff, pushing stuffing in with tweezers or tip of scissors. With toes pointing forwards, sew cast-off stitches of legs to lower edge of body.

Trousers

Sew up row ends of each leg of trousers from cast-on stitches to cast-off stitches at crotch. Sew round crotch and sew up row ends at centre back. Place trousers on doll and sew cast-off stitches to first row of upper body all the way round.

Skirt of Jacket and Belt

Join row ends of skirt of jacket and belt and with seam at centre back, place skirt of jacket on doll. Sew belt to body using backstitch on right side, all the way round.

Sleeves and Hands

Sew up row ends of hands and push a small ball of stuffing into hands using tweezers or tip of scissors. Sew up row ends of arms and stuff, pushing stuffing in with tweezers or tip of scissors. Gather round cast-on sts, pull tight and secure. Sew arms to doll at each side.

Features

Embroider Features as Girls and Boys on page 131. Using picture as a guide, work 3 buttons down front of jacket using white. Embroider buckle in gold using straight stitches (see page 139 for how to begin and fasten off the embroidery invisibly).

Hair

Work Hair as Girls and Boys on page 131.

Hat

Sew up row ends of hat and stuff top of hat. Pin hat to head, easing over forehead. Sew lower edge of hat to head, sewing through hair to head. Embroider strap in gold in chain stitch from one side of hat, around face and back up to hat (see page 139 for how to begin and fasten off the embroidery invisibly).

How to make Horse

Body
Using the thumb method and J, cast on 24 sts.
Row 1 and foll 2 alt rows: Purl.
Row 2 (RS): *(K1, m1) twice, k8, (m1, k1) twice, rep from * once (32 sts).
Row 4: *(K2, m1) twice, k8, (m1, k2) twice, rep from * once (40 sts).
Row 6: *(K3, m1) twice, k8, (m1, k3) twice, rep from * once (48 sts).
Beg with a p row, work 15 rows in st st.
Row 22: *(K1, k2tog) twice, k12, (k2tog, k1) twice, rep from * once (40 sts).
Row 23: Purl.
Row 24: *(K1, k2tog) twice, k8, (k2tog, k1) twice, rep from * once (32 sts).
Cast off p-wise.

Head
Using the thumb method and J, cast on 16 sts.
Row 1 and foll 2 alt rows: Purl.
Row 2 (RS): K6, (m1, k1) twice, (k1, m1) twice, k6 (20 sts).
Row 4: K8, (m1, k1) twice, (k1, m1) twice, k8 (24 sts).
Row 6: K10, (m1, k1) twice, (k1, m1) twice, k10 (28 sts).
Beg with a p row, work 3 rows in st st.
Row 10: K6, turn.
Row 11: S1p, p to end.

Row 12: Knit.
Row 13: P6, turn.
Row 14: S1k, k to end.
Beg with a p row, work 5 rows in st st.
Cast off 6 sts at beg of next 2 rows (16 sts).
Work 6 rows in st st.
Row 28: (K2tog) to end (8 sts).
Thread yarn through sts on needle, pull tight and secure by threading yarn a second time through sts.

Legs (make 4)
Beg at top edge using the thumb method and J, cast on 16 sts, WS facing to beg.
Beg with a p row, work 19 rows in st st.
Row 20: (K2tog) to end (8 sts).
Thread yarn through sts on needle, pull tight and secure by threading yarn a second time through sts.

Ears (make 2)
Using the thumb method and J, cast on 8 sts.
P 1 row then k 1 row.
Row 3 (WS): P1, (p2tog) 3 times, p1 (5 sts).
Thread yarn through sts on needle, pull tight and secure by threading yarn a second time through sts.

Making up
Tail
Cut 20 strands of yarn K, each 8in (20cm) approx and lay them in a bundle. Tie bundle around middle with a piece of yarn. Fold bundle in half.

Body
Fold cast-on stitches of body in half and sew up. Fold cast-off stitches in half and sew up. Sew up shaped row ends and enclose tail, sewing in place securely. Stuff body and sew up remainder of row ends.

Legs
Sew up row ends of legs and stuff legs. Sew four legs to lower edge of body. Trim ends of tail to 3in (7.5cm).

Head
Fold cast-on stitches of head in half and sew up. Sew up cast-on and cast-off stitches and sew up row ends beneath muzzle. Stuff head, pushing stuffing into muzzle. Leaving neck open, sew head to body.

Ears
Sew up row ends of each ear and sew ears to head.

Mane and Features
Using picture as a guide, embroider mane in dark brown using straight stitches. Embroider eyes on head in black, working a vertical chain stitch for each eye (see page 139 for how to begin and fasten off the embroidery invisibly).

MARY HAD A LITTLE LAMB

Information you'll need

Finished size

Mary measures 9in (23cm) high
Lamb measures 3½in (9cm) high

Materials

Any DK (US: light worsted) yarn
Note: Amounts are approximate
5g navy blue (A)
10g white (B)
10g pale pink (C)
10g cerise (D)
10g petrol blue (E)
10g brown (F)
5g beige (G)
5g oatmeal (H)
Oddments of black, red, pale pink
and dark brown for embroidery

1 pair of 3.25mm (UK10:US3) needles and
1 spare needle of the same size
Knitters' blunt-ended pins and a needle for
sewing up
Tweezers for stuffing small parts (optional)
Acrylic toy stuffing
Red pencil for shading cheeks

Tension

26 sts x 34 rows to 4in (10cm) square over
st st using 3.25mm needles and DK yarn
before stuffing.

Special abbreviation

M1: Pick up the horizontal loop between
the needles from front to back and work
into the back of it.

How to make Mary

Shoes, Socks, Legs, Body and Head

Right shoe, sock and leg

Beg at sole of shoe using the thumb method and A, cast on 14 sts.

Place a marker on cast-on edge between the 5th and 6th st of the sts just cast on.

Row 1 (WS): Purl.

Row 2: K2, (m1, k2) to end (20 sts).

Beg with a p row, work 5 rows in st st.

Shape shoe

Row 8: (K1, k2tog) twice, k2, (k2tog, k1) twice, k6 (16 sts).

Row 9: Purl.

Change to B for sock and dec:

Row 10: (K2, k2tog) twice, k8 (14 sts).

Beg with a p row, work 3 rows in st st.

Row 14: Purl.

Change to C for leg and beg with a p row, work 19 rows in st st.

Break yarn and set aside.

Left shoe, sock and leg

Beg at sole of shoe using the thumb method and A, cast on 14 sts.

Place a marker on cast-on edge between the 9th and 10th st of the sts just cast on.

Row 1 (WS): Purl.

Row 2: K2, (m1, k2) to end (20 sts).

Beg with a p row, work 5 rows in st st.

Shape shoe

Row 8: K7, (k2tog, k1) twice, (k1, k2tog) twice, k1 (16 sts).

Row 9: Purl.

Change to B for sock and dec:

Row 10: K8, (k2tog, k2) twice (14 sts).

Beg with a p row, work 3 rows in st st.

Row 14: Purl.

Change to C for leg and beg with a p row, work 19 rows in st st.

Join legs

Change to B for lower body and k across sts of left leg and then with the same yarn, cont knitting across sts of right leg (28 sts).

Beg with a p row, work 7 rows in st st.

Change to D for upper body and work 14 rows in st st.

Change to C for head and work 2 rows in st st.

Next row: *K4, (m1, k2) 4 times, k2, rep from * once (36 sts).

Beg with a p row, work 15 rows in st st.

Shape top of head

Next row: (K2tog, k2) to end (27 sts).

Next and foll alt row: Purl.

Next row: (K2tog, k1) to end (18 sts).

Next row: (K2tog) to end (9 sts).

Thread yarn through sts on needle and leave loose.

Sleeves, Arms and Hands (make 2)

Make Sleeves, Arms and Hands as Jack on page 34, using D for sleeve.

Cuffs (make 2)

Make Cuffs as Jack on page 35, using D.

Hair

Make Hair as Jack on page 35, using F.

Pinafore Dress

Beg at lower edge using the thumb method and E, cast on 54 sts and beg in garter st.

Work 2 rows in garter st.

Join on D for contrast stripe colour and beg with a k row, work 8 rows in st st in stripe, 2 rows D then 2 rows E, and do this alternately carrying yarn loosely up side of work.

Cont in stripe and dec:

Row 11 (RS): (K2tog, k4) to end (45 sts).

Beg with a p row, work 5 rows in stripe.

Cont in E and dec:

Row 17: (K2tog, k3) to end (36 sts).

Work 2 rows in garter st, ending with a RS row.

Cont in E and shape back and work bib as dungarees for Jack on page 35 from ** to end.

Straps (make 2)

Make Straps as Jack on page 35, using E.

Hat

Beg at brim using the thumb method and E, cast on 66 sts and beg in garter st. Work 2 rows in garter st.

Row 3 (RS): K1, (k2tog, k3) to end (53 sts).

Beg with a p row, work 3 rows in st st.

Row 7: K1, (k2tog, k2) to end (40 sts).

Beg with a p row, work 11 rows in st st.

Row 19: (K2tog, k3) to end (32 sts).

Row 20 and foll 2 alt rows: Purl.

Row 21: (K2tog, k2) to end (24 sts).

Row 23: (K2tog, k1) to end (16 sts).

Row 25: (K2tog) to end (8 sts).

Thread yarn through sts on needle, pull tight and secure by threading yarn a second time through sts.

Satchel

Using the thumb method and G, cast on 10 sts and beg in st st.

Beg with a k row, work 8 rows in st st.

Work 2 rows in garter st.

Beg with a k row, work 8 rows in st st.

Work 8 rows in garter st.

Row 27 (RS): K2tog, k to last 2 sts, k2tog tbl (8 sts).

Work 2 rows in garter st ending with a RS row.

Cast off in garter st.

Satchel Strap

Using the thumb method and G, cast on 50 sts, RS facing to beg.

Knit 1 row.

Cast off k-wise.

Making up

Shoes, Socks, Legs, Body and Head

Sew up row ends of shoes and with markers at tips of toes, oversew cast-on stitches; leg seam will be ¼in (6mm) on inside edge of heel. Sew up socks and place a ball of stuffing into toes. Sew up row ends of legs and sew round crotch. Stuff legs and sew up body seam. Stuff body and sew up row ends of head to halfway up head. Stuff head, pulling stitches on a thread tight at top of head and sew up remainder of row ends. To shape neck, take a double length of yarn to match upper body and sew a running stitch round last row of body, sewing in and out of every half stitch. Pull tight and knot yarn, sewing ends into neck.

Sleeves, Arms and Hands

Make up Sleeves, Arms and Hands as Jack on page 36.

Cuffs

Make up Cuffs as Jack on page 36.

Features

Embroider Features as Jack on page 36.

Hair

Make up Hair as Jack on page 36.

Plaits

Make two plaits in colour to match hair by cutting nine lengths of yarn for each plait, each 20in (50cm) long and lay them in a bundle. Tie a knot at centre of bundle and fold in half. Divide into three and plait for 2in (5cm) and tie a knot. Trim ends beyond knot to ½in (1.5cm) and sew plaits to hair at sides of head.

Pinafore and Straps

Sew up row ends of skirt of pinafore and with seam at centre back, place pinafore on doll. Sew cast-off stitches at waist to first row of upper body. Sew ends of straps to bib, take straps over shoulders, cross them over and sew ends to waist of pinafore at back.

Hat

Join row ends of hat and place on head and allow brim to roll up. Sew lower edge of hat to head all the way round.

Satchel and Strap

Fold front of satchel up and top of satchel over and sew up row ends. Using picture as a guide and using dark brown, embroider fastening at front of satchel. Sew strap to satchel and place on doll.

How to make Lamb

Body
Beg at lower edge using the thumb method and B, cast on 26 sts and work in rev st st.

Row 1 (RS): Purl.

Row 2: (K1, m1, k11, m1, k1) twice (30 sts).

Beg with a p row, work 13 rows in rev st st.

Row 16: K2tog, k11, (k2tog) twice, k11, k2tog tbl (26 sts).

Row 17: Purl.

Cast off in rev st st.

Legs (make 4)
Beg at top edge using the thumb method and H, cast on 10 sts.

Beg with a p row, work 7 rows in st st.

Row 8 (RS): K1, (k2tog, k1) to end (7 sts).

Thread yarn through sts on needle, pull tight and secure by threading yarn a second time through sts.

Head
Beg at top edge using the thumb method and B, cast on 11 sts and beg in rev st st.

Row 1 (RS): P2, (pfb, p2) to end (14 sts).

Beg with a k row, work 3 rows in rev st st. Change to H and continue in st st.

Row 5: (K1 tbl) to end.

Row 6 and foll alt row: Purl.

Row 7: K4, m1, k6, m1, k4 (16 sts).

Row 9: K4, m1, k8, m1, k4 (18 sts).

Beg with a p row, work 3 rows in st st.

Row 13: (K2tog, k1) to end (12 sts).

Row 14: Purl.

Row 15: (K2tog) to end (6 sts).

Thread yarn through sts on needle, pull tight and secure by threading yarn a second time through sts.

Ears (make 2)
Using the thumb method and B, cast on 7 sts.

Row 1 (RS): K2, k3tog, k2 (5 sts).

Cast off k-wise.

Tail
Using the thumb method and B, cast on 6 sts and work in rev st st.

Beg with a p row, work 3 rows in rev st st.

Row 4 (WS): (K2tog) twice, (kfb) twice (6 sts).

Work 3 rows in rev st st.

Thread yarn through sts on needle, pull tight and secure by threading yarn a second time through sts.

Making up

Body
Fold cast-on stitches of body in half and oversew. Fold cast-off stitches in half and oversew. Stuff body and sew up row ends.

Legs
Sew up row ends of legs and stuff legs, pushing stuffing in with tweezers or tip of scissors. Sew legs to body.

Head
Sew up row ends of head and stuff head, pushing stuffing in with tweezers or tip of scissors. With seam at centre back, oversew top edge. Pin and sew head to body.

Ears
Fold cast-off stitches of ears in half and sew up row ends. Sew ears to head at each side.

Tail
Sew up row ends of tail and sew one end of tail to body.

Features
Mark position of eyes on 3rd row below top of face with two clear knitted stitches in between. Embroider eyes in black and work a vertical chain stitch for each eye starting at marked position and ending one knitted row above the marked position. Using picture as a guide, embroider nose and mouth in black using straight stitches (see page 139 for how to begin and fasten off the embroidery invisibly).

LITTLE BOY BLUE

Information you'll need

Finished size
Boy measures 9in (23cm) high
Haystack measures 6½in (16.5cm) high
Sheep measures 4½in (11.5cm) high
Cow measures 5in (13cm) high

Materials
Any DK (US: light worsted) yarn
Note: Amounts are approximate
10g royal blue (A)
10g cream (B)
10g medium blue (C)
10g pale pink (D)
10g pale blue (E)
5g black (F)
10g pale brown (G)
5g golden cream (H)
5g beige (I)
50g lemon (J)
50g gold (K)
10g white (L)
5g peach (M)
10g terracotta (N)
5g biscuit (O)
Oddments of black, red, pale pink
and grey for embroidery

1 pair of 3.25mm (UK10:US3) knitting
needles and a spare needle of the same size
Knitters' blunt-ended pins and a needle
for sewing up
Tweezers for stuffing small parts (optional)
Acrylic toy stuffing
Red pencil for shading cheeks

Tension
26 sts x 34 rows to 4in (10cm) square over
st st using 3.25mm needles and DK yarn
before stuffing.

Special abbreviation
M1: Pick up the horizontal loop between
the needles from front to back and work
into the back of it.

Row 10: K5, (k2tog, k2) twice, k3 (14 sts).
Beg with a p row, work 21 rows in st st.
Cast off.

Breeches and Belt
Right Leg
Beg at lower edge using the thumb
method and E, cast on 20 sts.
Row 1 (RS): Purl.
Beg with a p row, work 15 rows in st st.
Cast off 2 sts at beg of next 2 rows
(16 sts).
Break yarn and set aside.
Left Leg
Work as right leg but do not break yarn.
Join legs
With RS facing, k across sts of left leg and
then with the same yarn, cont knitting
across sts of right leg (32 sts).
Beg with a p row, work 3 rows in st st.
Change to F for belt and work 3 rows
in garter st, ending with a RS row.
Cast off in garter st.

Sleeves and Hands (make 2)
Make Sleeves and Hands as Jack on page
34, using C for sleeves.

Cuffs (make 2)
Make Cuffs as Jack on page 35, using C.

Hair
Make Hair as Jack on page 35, using G.

Waistcoat
Make Waistcoat as Master on page 42,
using A.

Cap
Beg at lower edge using the thumb
method and E, cast on 36 sts.
Rows 1 and 2: P 2 rows.

How to make Boy Blue
Body and Head
Using the thumb method and B for lower
body, cast on 28 sts.
Place a marker at centre of cast-on edge.
Beg with a p row, work 7 rows in st st.
Change to C for upper body and work 14
rows in st st.
Change to D for head and work 2 rows in
st st.
**Next row (RS): *K4, (m1, k2) 4 times,
k2, rep from * once (36 sts).
Beg with a p row, work 15 rows in st st.
Shape top of head
Next row: (K2tog, k2) to end (27 sts).
Next and foll alt row: Purl.
Next row: (K2tog, k1) to end (18 sts).

Next row: (K2tog) to end (9 sts).
Thread yarn through sts on needle,
pull tight and secure by threading yarn
a second time through sts.

Shoes and Legs (make 2)
Beg at sole of shoe using the thumb
method and A, cast on 14 sts.
Row 1 (WS): Purl.
Row 2: K2, (m1, k2) to end (20 sts).
Beg with a p row, work 5 rows in st st.
Shape shoe
Row 8: K4, (k2tog, k1) twice, (k1, k2tog)
twice, k4 (16 sts).
Row 9: Purl.
Change to B for leg and dec:

Row 3 (RS): K1, (m1, k2) to last st, m1, k1 (54 sts).

Beg with a p row, work 7 rows in st st.

Row 11: (K2tog, k4) to end (45 sts).

Row 12 and foll 3 alt rows: Purl.

Row 13: (K2tog, k3) to end (36 sts).

Row 15: (K2tog, k2) to end (27sts).

Row 17: (K2tog, k1) to end (18 sts).

Row 19: (K2tog) to end (9 sts).

Thread yarn through sts on needle, pull tight and secure by threading yarn a second time through sts.

Peak

Using the thumb method and E, cast on 12 sts.

Row 1 (WS): Purl.

Row 2: (K2, m1) twice, k4, (m1, k2) twice (16 sts).

Beg with a p row, work 5 rows in st st.

Row 8: K1, k2tog (k2, k2tog) 3 times, k1 (12 sts).

Cast off p-wise.

Horn

Using the thumb method and H, cast on 6 sts and beg in st st.

Row 1 (WS): Purl.

Row 2: K1, m1, k to last st, m1, k1 (8 sts).

Row 3: Purl.

Row 4: Knit.

Row 5: Purl.

Rows 6 to 13: Rep rows 2 to 5 twice (12 sts).

Rows 14 and 15: Rep rows 2 and 3 once (14 sts).

Work 4 rows in garter st.

Change to I and k 1 row.

Row 21: (P2tog) to end (7 sts).

Thread yarn through sts on needle, pull tight and secure by threading yarn a second time through sts.

Making up

Body and Head

Sew up row ends of head and body and stuff. With seam at centre back, bring seam and marker together and sew up cast-on stitches. To shape neck, take a double length of yarn to match upper body and sew a running stitch round last row of body, sewing in and out of every half stitch. Pull tight and knot yarn, sewing ends into neck.

Shoes and Legs

Fold cast-on stitches of shoes in half and sew up. Sew up row ends of shoes and place a ball of stuffing into toes. Sew up row ends of legs and stuff legs. With seam of each leg at centre back, sew across cast-off stitches. With toes pointing forwards, sew cast-off stitches of legs to cast-on stitches of body at lower edge.

Breeches and Belt

Make up Breeches and Belt as Master on page 42.

Sleeves and Hands

Make up Sleeves and Hands as Jack on page 34.

Cuffs

Make up Cuffs as Jack on page 36.

Features

Start and finish off features at top of head under hair. Embroider closed eyes in black as shown in picture, marking their position on the 9th and 10th rows of head over two stitches with two clear stitches in between. Embroider mouth in red on the 4th and 5th rows below eyes making a shallow 'v' shape across three stitches. Embroider nose in D at centre front on row between eyes, making a bundle of five horizontal stitches over one stitch. Shade cheeks with a red pencil. Embroider buckle in grey, taking a horizontal stitch above and below belt, and join these with a double stitch at each side to form a rectangle (see page 139 for how to begin and fasten off the embroidery invisibly).

Hair

Make up Hair as Jack on page 36.

Waistcoat

Make up Waistcoat as Master on page 42.

Cap and Peak

Sew up row ends of cap and stuff around inside corners of cap with no stuffing at crown. Place cap on head and pin and sew lower edge of cap to head all the way round. With right side of stocking stitch outside, fold peak, bringing cast-on and cast-off stitches together, and sew up these stitches. Gather round row ends of peak at each side, pull tight and secure. Sew peak to lower edge of cap at centre front.

Horn and Strap

To make strap, make a twisted cord out of two strands of yarn, starting with each strand 60in (150cm) long (see page 139). Fold twisted cord in half and tie a knot 4½in (11.5cm) from folded end. Trim ends beyond knot. Sew up row ends of horn from stitches pulled tight on a thread to halfway up horn and stuff horn, pushing stuffing in with tweezers or tip of scissors. Finish sewing up row ends and enclose knot of strap in this seam ½in (1cm) below tip of narrow end. To curl horn, sew a gathering stitch along seam and pull to curl horn and sew back along this seam to secure.

How to make Haystack

Note: Haystack and base are knitted throughout using one strand of K and one strand of J together, treated as one strand.

Haystack

Beg at lower edge using the thumb method and K and J, cast on 80 sts and work in garter st.

Work 28 rows in garter st.

Row 29 (RS): (K1, k2tog, k14, k2tog, k1) 4 times (72 sts).

Work 15 rows in garter st.

Row 45: (K1, k2tog, k12, k2tog, k1) 4 times (64 sts).

Work 15 rows in garter st.

Row 61: (K1, k2tog, k10, k2tog, k1) 4 times (56 sts).

Work 5 rows in garter st.

Row 67: (K1, k2tog, k8, k2tog, k1) 4 times (48 sts).

Work 3 rows in garter st.

Shape top

Row 71: (K2tog, k8, k2tog) 4 times (40 sts).

Row 72 and foll 3 alt rows: Knit.

Row 73: (K2tog, k6, k2tog) 4 times (32 sts).

Row 75: (K2tog, k4, k2tog) 4 times (24 sts).

Row 77: (K2tog, k2, k2tog) 4 times (16 sts).

Row 79: (K2tog) to end (8 sts).

Row 80: Knit.

Thread yarn through sts on needle, pull tight and secure by threading yarn a second time through sts.

Base

Using the thumb method and K and J, cast on 25 sts and work in garter st, RS facing to beg.

Work 45 rows in garter st.

Cast off in garter st.

Making up
Haystack and Base

Sew up row ends of haystack and stuff with plenty of stuffing. Pin and sew base to lower edge of haystack all the way round.

How to make Sheep

Make up Sheep as Black Sheep on pages 47–8, using L for Body, M for Legs; beg with L for Head and change to M for Face, M for Ears and L for Tail. Embroider features in black.

How to make Cow

Body

Beg at lower edge using the thumb method and N, cast on 32 sts.

First and foll 2 alt rows: Purl.

Row 2 (RS): (K1, m1, k1, m1, k12, m1, k1, m1, k1) twice (40 sts).

Row 4: (K1, m1, k2, m1, k14, m1, k2, m1, k1) twice (48 sts).

Row 6: (K1, m1, k3, m1, k16, m1, k3, m1, k1) twice (56 sts).

Beg with a p row, work 19 rows in st st.

Row 26: (K2tog) twice, k20, (k2tog) 4 times, k20, (k2tog) twice (48 sts).

Row 27 and foll alt row: Purl.

Row 28: (K2tog) twice, k16, (k2tog) 4 times, k16, (k2tog) twice (40 sts).

Row 30: (K2tog) twice, k12, (k2tog) 4 times, k12, (k2tog) twice (32 sts).

Cast off p-wise.

Legs (make 4)

Beg at top edge using the thumb method and N, cast on 19 sts.

Row 1 (WS): P12, turn.

Row 2: S1k, k4, turn.

Row 3: S1p, p to end.

Work 12 rows in st st.

Row 16: K1, (k2tog, k1) to end (13 sts).

Cast off p-wise.

Head

Beg at lower edge using the thumb method and O, cast on 22 sts.

Row 1 (WS): Purl.

Row 2: K5, (m1, k1) 5 times, k3, (m1, k1) 5 times, k4 (32 sts).

Beg with a p row, work 5 rows in st st.

Row 8: K4, (k2tog, k1) 3 times, k7, (k2tog, k1) 3 times, k3 (26 sts).

Change to N.

Row 9: Purl.

Row 10: (K1 tbl) to end.

Beg with a p row, work 7 rows in st st.

Row 18: (K4, k2tog, k1, k2tog, k4) twice (22 sts).

Row 19 and foll 2 alt rows: Purl.

Row 20: (K3, k2tog, k1, k2tog, k3) twice (18 sts).

Row 22: (K2, k2tog, k1, k2tog, k2) twice (14 sts).

Row 24: (K1, k2tog, k1, k2tog, k1) twice (10 sts).

Thread yarn through sts on needle, pull tight and secure by threading yarn a second time through sts.

Large patch (make 2)

Using the thumb method and G, cast on 4 sts and work in garter st.

Row 1 (RS): Knit.

Row 2: K1, m1, k to last 2 sts, m1, k1 (6 sts).

Rows 3 and 4: Rep rows 1 and 2 once (8 sts).

Work 5 rows in garter st.

Row 10: K1, m1, k to last 2 sts, m1, k1 (10 sts).

Row 11: Knit.

Rows 12 and 13: Rep rows 10 and 11 once (12 sts).

Work 9 rows in garter st.

Row 23: (K2tog) twice, k4, k2tog, k2tog tbl (8 sts).

Row 24: Knit.

Row 25: (K2tog) 4 times (4 sts).

Cast off in garter st.

Small patch

Using the thumb method and G, cast on 4 sts and work in garter st.

Row 1 (RS): Knit.

Row 2: K1, m1, k to last 2 sts, m1, k1 (6 sts).

Row 3: Knit.

Row 4: As row 2 (8 sts).

Work 12 rows in garter st.

Row 17: K2tog, k4, k2tog tbl (6 sts).

Row 18: Knit.

Row 19: K2tog, k2, k2tog tbl (4 sts).

Cast off in garter st.

Ears (make 2)

Using the thumb method and N, cast on 14 sts and work in garter st.

Garter st 2 rows.

Row 3 (RS): K4, (k3tog) twice, k4 (10 sts).

Cast off in garter st.

Making up

Tail
Make a twisted cord out of 6 strands of yarn N, each 24in (60cm) long (see page 139). Tie a knot 2in (5cm) from folded end and trim ends beyond knot to ½in (1.5cm).

Body
Fold cast-on stitches of body in half and sew up, fold cast-off stitches in half and sew up. Sew up shaped row ends and insert tail and attach securely. Stuff body and finish sewing up row ends.

Legs
Fold cast-off stitches of legs in half and sew up. Sew up straight row ends and stuff legs. Pin and sew legs to body.

Head
Sew up row ends of head and stuff. With this seam at centre back, sew up lower edge.

Patches
Using picture as a guide, sew a small patch to head and large patches to body at front and back using backstitch, all the way round outside edge of patches.

Ears
Fold cast-off stitches of ears in half and sew up. Gather row ends of each ear, pull tight and secure. Sew ears to head at each side.

Features
Mark position of eyes on 4th row above muzzle with three clear knitted stitches in between. Embroider eyes in black and work a vertical chain stitch for each eye starting at marked position and finishing on second row above marked position. Work nostrils in the same way on muzzle with six clear knitted stitches in between and finishing on the row above (see page 139 for how to begin and fasten off the embroidery invisibly). Pin and sew head to cow.

MARY, MARY, QUITE CONTRARY

Information you'll need

Finished size
Mary measures 9in (23cm) high
Garden measures 8in (20cm) across

Materials
Any DK (US: light worsted) yarn
Note: Amounts are approximate
10g orange (A)
5g white (B)
10g pale pink (C)
10g gold (D)
10g brown (E)
10g grey (F)
25g emerald green (G)
5g buttermilk (H)
5g silver grey (I)
10g dark green (J)
10g mid green (K)
5g pink (L)
5g yellow (M)
Oddments of black, red and pale pink
for embroidery
1 pair of 3.25mm (UK10: US3) needles
and 1 spare needle of the same size
Knitters' blunt-ended pins and a needle
for sewing up
Tweezers for stuffing small parts (optional)

Acrylic toy stuffing
Red pencil for shading cheeks
Pipe cleaner
8 plastic drinking straws

Tension
26 sts x 34 rows to 4in (10cm) square over
st st using 3.25mm needles and DK yarn
before stuffing.

Special abbreviation
M1: Pick up the horizontal loop between
the needles from front to back and work
into the back of it.

How to make Mary

Shoes, Socks, Legs, Body and Head
Make Shoes, Socks, Legs, Body and Head as Mary had a Little Lamb on page 62, using A for shoes, B for lower body and D for upper body.

Sleeves, Arms and Hands (make 2)
Work Sleeves, Arms and Hands as Jill on page 37, using D for sleeve.

Hair
Make Hair as Jack on page 35, using E.

Pinafore Dress and Straps
Make Pinafore Dress and Straps as Mary on pages 63–4, using A and joining on D for contrast stripe colour. Make Straps in A.

Hat
Make Hat as Mary on page 64, using D.

Watering Can
Beg at base using the thumb method and F, cast on 8 sts.
Row 1 and foll alt row: Purl.
Row 2 (RS): (Kfb) to end 16 sts.
Row 4: (Kfb, k1) to end 24 sts.
Rows 5 to 9: Purl.
Beg with a k row, work 2 rows in st st.
Row 12: (K2, k2tog, k4, k2tog, k2) twice (20 sts).
Beg with a p row, work 5 rows in st st.
Row 18: (K2, k2tog, k2, k2tog, k2) twice (16 sts).

Row 19: Purl.
Work 3 rows in garter st.
Row 23: Purl.
Row 24: (K2tog) to end (8 sts).
Thread yarn through sts on needle, pull tight and secure by threading yarn a second time through sts.

Rim of Watering Can
Using the thumb method and F, cast on 22 sts, RS facing to beg.
K 1 row.
Cast off k-wise.

Spout
Using the thumb method and F, cast on 10 sts.
P 1 row then k 2 rows then p 1 row.

Row 5 (RS): (K2tog) to end (5 sts).
Row 6: Purl.
Row 7: K1, m1, k3, m1, k1 (7 sts).
Beg with a p row, work 3 rows in st st.
Row 11: K3, m1, k1, m1, k3 (9 sts).
Row 12 and foll 2 alt rows: Purl.
Row 13: K2tog, k1, m1, k3, m1, k1, k2tog tbl (9 sts).
Row 15: K2tog, k to last 2 sts, k2tog tbl (7 sts).
Row 17: As row 15 (5 sts).
Cast off p-wise.

Handle
Using the thumb method and F, cast on 18 sts, WS facing to beg.
Beg with a p row, work 4 rows in st st, ending with a k row.
Cast off p-wise.

Making up

Doll
Make up doll as Mary on page 65, omitting plaits and satchel.

Bunches
Take yarn to match hair and wind it round and round 4 fingers 25 times. Cut all strands and lay out flat. You will now have a bundle of 25 strands 6in (15cm) approx in length. Tie this bundle in the middle and fold in half. Cut ends to 2in (5cm) from folded end. Repeat for second bunch and sew bunches to hair at sides.

Watering Can
Gather round cast-on stitches of watering can, pull tight and secure. Sew up row ends of watering can, leaving a gap, then stuff and sew up gap.

Rim of Watering Can
Sew up row ends of rim and sew lower edge around top of watering can.

Spout
Gather round cast-on stitches of spout, pull tight and secure. Sew up row ends of spout, leaving last five rows open, and stuff, pushing stuffing in with tweezers or tip of scissors. Sew spout to watering can.

Handle
Take the pipe cleaner and fold in half then cut to length of handle. Join cast-on and cast-off stitches of handle, enclosing pipe cleaner inside. Curve handle and sew ends to watering can.

How to make Garden

Pretty Maids (make 5)
Beg at back of flower using the thumb method and J, cast on 7 sts.
Row 1: Purl.
Row 2 (RS): (Kfb) to end (14 sts).
Change to L and p 1 row.
Row 4: (Kfb, k1) to end (21 sts).
P 1 row then k 1 row.
Picot edge: K1, (yf, k2tog) to end.
K 1 row then p 1 row.
Change to M and k 1 row.
Row 11: (P2tog, p1) to end (14 sts).
Row 12: (K2tog) to end (7 sts).
Thread yarn through sts on needle, pull tight and secure by threading yarn a second time through sts.

Stem (make 5)
Using the thumb method and J, cast on 5 sts and work in rev st st, RS facing to beg.
Beg with a p row, rev st st for 4½in (11.5cm).
Cast off.

Leaves (make 6)
Using the thumb method and J, cast on 3 sts.
Row 1 (WS): Purl.
Row 2: K1, (m1, k1) to end (5 sts).
Rows 3 and 4: Rep rows 1 and 2 once (9 sts).
Row 5: Purl.
Row 6: K2, (m1, k1) twice, k2, (m1, k1) twice, k1 (13 sts).
Beg with a p row, work 7 rows in st st.
Row 14: K2, k3tog, k3, k3tog, k2 (9 sts).
Beg with a p row, work 3 rows in st st.
Row 18: K1, (k3tog, k1) twice (5 sts).
Row 19: Purl.
Thread yarn through sts on needle, pull tight and secure by threading yarn a second time through sts.

mary, mary, quite contrary

Row 10: (K2, m1) twice, k3, (m1, k2) twice (15 sts).
P 1 row then k 1 row.
Picot edge: K1, (yf, k2tog) to end.
K 1 row then p 1 row.
Row 16: (K1, k2tog) twice, k3, (k2tog, k1) twice (11 sts).
Rows 17 to 19: Rep rows 7 to 9 once.
Row 20: K1, m1, (k2tog) twice, k1, (k2tog) twice, m1, k1 (9 sts).
Row 21: Purl.
Row 22: (K2tog) twice, k1, k2tog, k2tog tbl (5 sts).
Row 23: Purl.
Cast off.

Garden

Using the thumb method and G, cast on 40 sts and work in garter st, RS facing to beg.
Garter st 41 rows.
Cast off in garter st.

Back wall

Using the thumb method and G, cast on 40 sts and work in garter st, RS facing to beg.
Garter st 35 rows.
Cast off in garter st.

Side Walls (make 2)

Using the thumb method and G, cast on 20 sts and work in garter st.
Garter st 4 rows.
Row 5 (RS): K18, turn.
Row 6: S1k, k to end.
Row 7: K15, turn.
Row 8: S1k, k to end.
Row 9: K12, turn.
Row 10: S1k, k to end.
Row 11: K9, turn.
Row 12: S1k, k to end.
Row 13: K6, turn.

Silver Bells (make 6)

Using the thumb method and I, cast on 4 sts.
Row 1 (WS): Purl.
Row 2: K1, (m1, k1) to end (7 sts).
Rows 3 and 4: Rep rows 1 and 2 once (13 sts).
Beg with a p row, work 4 rows in st st, ending on a k row (this part is turned under).
Picot edge: K1, (yf, k2tog) to end.
Beg with a k row, work 4 rows in st st.
Row 14: K1, (k2tog, k2) to end (10 sts).
Row 15: Purl.
Row 16: K1, (k2tog, k1) to end (7 sts).
Thread yarn through sts on needle, pull tight and secure by threading yarn a second time through sts.

Stem (make 3)

Make Stem as stem of Pretty Maids, using K, working in rev st st for 2½in (6cm).

Leaves (make 6)

Make Leaves as leaves of Pretty Maids, using K.

Cockle Shells (make 4)

Using the thumb method and H, cast on 5 sts.
Beg with a p row, work 3 rows in st st.
Row 4 (RS): K2, m1, k1, m1, k2 (7 sts).
Row 5: Purl.
Row 6: K2, (m1, k1) 4 times, k1 (11 sts).
Row 7: P8, turn.
Row 8: S1k, k4, turn.
Row 9: S1p, p to end.

Row 14: S1k, k to end.
Row 15: K3, turn.
Row 16: S1k, k to end.
Garter st 4 rows.
Row 21: K3, turn.
Row 22: S1k, k to end.
Row 23: K6, turn.
Row 24: S1k, k to end.
Row 25: K9, turn.
Row 26: S1k, k to end.
Row 27: K12, turn.
Row 28: S1k, k to end.
Row 29: K15, turn.
Row 30: S1k, k to end.
Row 31: K18, turn.
Row 32: S1k, k to end.
Garter st 3 rows.
Cast off in garter st.

Making up

Pretty Maids, Stems and Leaves

Gather round cast-on stitches of flower, pull tight and secure. Join row ends of flower and press flat. Cut five lengths of plastic drinking straw, each 4in (10cm) long. Sew up row ends of stem around straw and gather round top and bottom, pull tight and secure. Sew a flower to top of each stem. Sew up row ends of leaves and with this seam at centre back, sew leaves to flower stems.

Silver Bells, Stems and Leaves

Sew up row ends of bells and turn lower edge under and secure with a stitch. Cut three lengths of plastic drinking straw, each 2in (5cm) long. Make up stems and leaves as pretty maids, sewing leaves to base of each stem.

Cockle Shells

Bring cast-on and cast-off stitches of cockle shells together and sew up. Push a tiny ball of stuffing inside and sew up row ends.

Garden and Garden Walls

Bring cast-on and cast-off stitches of garden walls together and sew up. Push a little stuffing inside and sew up row ends. Sew long row ends of two side walls to ends of back wall and sew walls to garden. Using picture as a guide, sew pretty maids, silver bells and cockle shells to garden.

LITTLE MISS MUFFET

Information you'll need

Finished size
Miss Muffet measures 9in (23cm) high
Spider measures 4in (10cm) across
Tuffet measures 4in (10cm) across

Materials
Any DK (US: light worsted) yarn
Note: Amounts are approximate
5g yellow (A)
10g pale pink (B)
10g white (C)
15g red (D)
10g brown (E)
20g apple green (F)
20g moss green (G)
5g blue (H)
5g buttermilk (I)
5g silver grey (J)
10g black (K)
Oddments of black, red, bright
green, silver grey and pale pink
for embroidery
1 pair of 3.25mm (UK10:US3)
knitting needles
Knitters' blunt-ended pins
and a needle for sewing up
Acrylic toy stuffing
Red pencil for shading cheeks

Tension
26 sts x 34 rows to 4in (10cm) square
over st st using 3.25mm needles and
DK yarn before stuffing.

Special abbreviation
M1: Pick up the horizontal loop between
the needles from front to back and work
into the back of it.

How to make
Miss Muffet
Body and Head
Using the thumb method and C for lower body, cast on 28 sts, WS facing to beg. Place a marker at centre of cast-on sts. Beg with a p row, work 7 rows in st st.
Change to D for upper body and work 10 rows in st st.
Change to B for neck and work 4 rows in st st.
Place a marker on last row for neck gathering.
Work 2 rows in st st.
Work head as Boy Blue on page 70 from ** to end.

Slippers and Legs (make 2)

Beg at sole of slipper using the thumb method and A, cast on 14 sts.

Row 1 (WS): Purl.

Row 2: K2, (m1, k2) to end (20 sts).

Beg with a p row, work 3 rows in st st. Change to B for leg and work 2 rows in st st.

Shape foot

Row 8: K4, (k2tog, k1) twice, (k1, k2tog) twice, k4 (16 sts).

Row 9: Purl.

Row 10: K5, (k2tog, k2) twice, k3 (14 sts).

Beg with a p row, work 21 rows in st st. Cast off.

Skirt of Dress

Beg at lower edge using the thumb method and C, cast on 54 sts.

P 1 row then k 1 row (this part is turned under).

Picot row (WS): K2, (yf, k2tog) to end.

Beg with a k row, work 2 rows in st st. Change to A and work 2 rows in garter st. Change to D and beg with a k row, work 18 rows in st st.

Row 26: (K2tog, k4) to end (45 sts).

Beg with a p row, work 3 rows in st st.

Row 30: (K2tog, k3) to end (36 sts).

Cast off p-wise.

Sleeves, Arms and Hands (make 2)

Make Sleeves, Arms and Hands as Dame on pages 44–5, using D for sleeve.

Sleeve Frills (make 2)

Using the thumb method and C, cast on 20 sts.

P 1 row then k 1 row (this part is turned under).

Picot row (WS): K2, (yf, k2tog) to end.

Beg with a k row, work 2 rows in st st. Change to A and k 1 row. Cast off k-wise.

Neck Band

Using the thumb method and D, cast on 36 sts, RS facing to beg. Cast off p-wise.

Hair

Make Hair as Jack on page 35, using E.

Bun and Hair loops

Make Bun and Hair loops as Dame on page 45, using E.

Hair Flowers

Make Hair Flowers as Dame on page 45, using A.

Making up

Body and Head

Sew up row ends of head and body and stuff. With seam at centre back, bring seam and marker together and sew up cast-on stitches. To shape neck, take a double length of B and sew a running stitch round row with marker at neck, sewing in and out of every half stitch. Pull tight and knot yarn, sewing ends into neck.

Slippers and Legs

Fold cast-on stitches of slippers in half and sew up. Sew up row ends of slippers and place a ball of stuffing into toes. Sew up row ends of legs and stuff legs. With seam of each leg at centre back of legs, sew across cast-off stitches. With toes pointing forwards, sew cast-off stitches of legs to cast-on stitches of body at lower edge.

Skirt of Dress

Turn hem under and sew in place. Sew up row ends of skirt of dress. Place skirt of dress on doll and sew cast-off stitches to first row of upper body all the way round.

Hands, Arms and Sleeves

Make up Hands, Arms and Sleeves as Dame on page 46.

Sleeve Frills

Turn hem under and sew in place. Place sleeve frills around arms and sew up row ends. Sew cast-off stitches of sleeve frills to first row of sleeve all the way round. Sew arms to doll at either side, sewing cast-on stitches at top of arms to second row below neck.

Neck Band

Make up Neck Band as Dame on page 46.

Features

Embroider eyes and nose as Jack on page 36. Embroider a startled mouth in red on 2nd to 4th rows below nose, taking 3 vertical stitches in a bundle. Shade cheeks with a red pencil.

Hair

Make up Hair as Jack on page 36.

Bun

Make up Bun as Dame on page 46.

Hair Loops and Flowers

Make up Hair Loops and Flowers as Dame on page 46.

How to make Bowl and Spoon

Bowl

Note: Before beg, cut a piece of C 80in (200cm) in length and reserve.

Beg at centre of inside of bowl using the thumb method and C (main ball), cast on 8 sts.

Row 1 and foll alt row: Purl.
Row 2 (RS): (Kfb) to end (16 sts).
Row 4: (Kfb, k1) to end (24 sts).
Beg with a p row, work 3 rows in st st. Work 6 rows in garter st.
Join on H and reserved piece of C and work in stripe, carrying yarn loosely up sides of work and work in patt as foll:
Row 14: Using H, knit.
Rows 15 and 16: Using C (reserved piece), beg with a p row, work 2 rows in st st, ending on a k row.
Row 17: Using H, purl.
Cont in C and work 2 rows in st st.
Row 20: (K2tog, k1) to end (16 sts).
Row 21: Purl.
Row 22: (K2tog) to end (8 sts).
Thread yarn through sts on needle, pull tight and secure by threading yarn a second time through sts.

Curds and Whey

Using the thumb method and I, cast on 2 sts and work in moss st.
Row 1 (RS): (Kfb) twice (4 sts).
Row 2: (P1, k1) twice.
Row 3: Kfb, p1, k1, kfb (6 sts).
Row 4: (K1, p1) to end.
Row 5: (P1, k1) to end.
Rows 6 and 7: Rep rows 4 and 5, once.
Row 8: As row 4.
Row 9: K2tog, p1, k1, p2tog (4 sts).
Row 10: (P1, k1) twice.
Cast off in moss st.

Spoon

Using the thumb method and J,
cast on 12 sts.

Row 1 (WS): S1p, p4 turn.
Row 2: S1k, k to end.
Row 3: S1p, p5, turn.
Row 4: S1k, k to end.
Row 5: P across all sts.
Row 6: Knit.
Rows 7 and 8: Rep rows 5 and 6 once.
Rows 9 and 10: Rep rows 3 and 4 once.
Rows 11 and 12: Rep rows 1 and 2 once.
Row 13: Purl.
Cast off loosely.

Making up

Bowl

With right sides of stocking stitch outside,
sew up row ends of bowl. Assemble lining
into inside of bowl and sew through centre
of bowl to underneath to secure in place.

Curds and Whey

Place a small ball of stuffing into bowl and
sew outer edge of curds and whey to 2nd
row below rim of inside of bowl, leaving
a gap. Add more stuffing and complete
the sewing of outer edge.

Spoon

With right sides of stocking stitch outside,
sew up cast-on and cast-off stitches of
bowl of spoon; this seam will be at centre
back. Sew up row ends at top edge. Fold
pipe cleaner in half and insert into wrong
side of handle of spoon and join cast-on
and cast-off stitches of handle around
pipe cleaner. Trim excess pipe cleaner then
gather round row ends at top and bottom
of spoon, pull tight and secure. To shape
bowl of spoon, sew a gathering stitch
round outside edge of bowl of spoon,
pull to curve spoon and fasten off.
Sew spoon to right hand of doll.

little miss muffet

How to make Tuffet

Note: Tuffet is knitted throughout using 1 strand of F and 1 strand of G together, treated as one strand.

Beg at lower edge using the thumb method and F and G, cast on 64 sts and work in garter st.

Work 12 rows in garter st.

Row 13 (RS): K1, (k2tog, k7) to end (57 sts).

Work 3 rows in garter st.

Row 17: K1, (k2tog, k6) to end (50 sts).

Row 18 and foll 5 alt rows: Knit.

Row 19: K1, (k2tog, k5) to end (43 sts).

Row 21: K1, (k2tog, k4) to end (36 sts).

Row 23: K1, (k2tog, k3) to end (29 sts).

Row 25: K1, (k2tog, k2) to end (22 sts).

Row 27: K1, (k2tog, k1) to end (15 sts).

Row 29: K1, (k2tog) to end (8 sts).

Thread yarn through sts on needle, pull tight and secure by threading yarn a second time through sts.

Base

Beg at outside edge using the thumb method and F and G, cast on 64 sts and work in garter st.

Row 1 (RS): K1, (k2tog, k7) to end (57 sts).

Row 2 and foll 6 alt rows: Knit.

Row 3: K1, (k2tog, k6) to end (50 sts).

Row 5: K1, (k2tog, k5) to end (43 sts).

Row 7: K1, (k2tog, k4) to end (36 sts).

Row 9: K1, (k2tog, k3) to end (29 sts).

Row 11: K1, (k2tog, k2) to end (22 sts).

Row 13: K1, (k2tog, k1) to end (15 sts).

Row 15: K1, (k2tog) to end (8 sts).

Thread yarn through sts on needle, pull tight and secure by threading yarn a second time through sts.

Making up

Tuffet

Sew up row ends of tuffet and stuff with plenty of stuffing.

Base

Sew up row ends of base and pin and sew cast-on stitches of base to cast-on stitches of tuffet all the way round, adding more stuffing if needed.

How to make Spider
Body
Beg at middle of base using the thumb method and K, cast on 8 sts.

Row 1 and foll 2 alt rows: Purl.
Row 2 (RS): (Kfb) to end (16 sts).
Row 4: (Kfb, k1) to end (24 sts).
Row 6: (Kfb, k2) to end (32 sts).
Beg with a p row, work 3 rows in st st.
Row 10: (K2tog, k2) to end (24 sts).
Row 11 and foll alt row: Purl.
Row 12: (K2tog, k1) to end (16 sts).
Row 14: (K2tog) to end (8 sts).
Thread yarn through sts on needle and leave loose.

Legs (make 8)
Using the thumb method and K, cast on 10 sts.

Row 1 (WS): P4, (pfb) twice, p4 (12 sts).
Row 2: Knit.
Row 3: P4, (p2tog) twice, p4 (10 sts).
Cast off k-wise.

Making up
String
Make a twisted cord out of one piece of yarn K, starting with the yarn 50in (130cm) long. Tie a knot 16in (40cm) from folded end and trim ends beyond knot.

Body
Insert knot of string into centre of stitches on a thread. Pull stitches on a thread tight and secure and sew through knot on wrong side. Sew up row ends of body, leaving a gap. Stuff body and gather round cast-on stitches, and pull tight and secure and sew up gap.

Legs
Sew up cast-on and cast off stitches of each leg, sewing along leg. Sew legs to spider, four to each side.

Features
Using picture as a guide, mark position of eyes on spider and work two eyes in green, taking a small vertical chain stitch. Embroider mouth in silver grey, taking two straight stitches (see page 139 for how to begin and fasten off the embroidery invisibly).

HICKORY, DICKORY, DOCK

Information you'll need

Finished size
Clock stands 8in (20cm) high
Mouse measures 2in (5cm) long,
excluding tail

Materials
Any DK (US: light worsted) yarn
Note: Amounts are approximate
50g light brown (A)
5g dark brown (B)
5g oatmeal (C)
5g white (D)
5g pink (E)
Oddments of black and pink
for embroidery

1 pair of 3.25mm (UK10:US3) needles
Knitters' blunt-ended pins and a needle
for sewing up
Tweezers for stuffing small parts (optional)
Acrylic toy stuffing

Tension
26 sts x 34 rows to 4in (10cm) square over
st st using 3.25mm needles and DK yarn
before stuffing.

Special abbreviation
M1: Pick up the horizontal loop between
the needles from front to back and work
into the back of it.

How to make Clock

Base (make 6 pieces)
Using the thumb method and A, cast on 17 sts.
Beg with a p row, work 5 rows in st st.
Row 6 (RS): K4, (p1, k1) 5 times, k3.
Row 7: Purl.
Row 8: K4, p1, k7, p1, k4.
Row 9: Purl.
Rows 10 to 17: Rep rows 8 and 9, 4 times more.
Row 18: As row 6.
Beg with a p row, work 5 rows in st st.
Cast off.

Middle Section (make 4 pieces)
Using the thumb method and A, cast on 11 sts.
Beg with a p row, work 3 rows in st st.
Row 4 (RS): K3, (p1, k1) 3 times, k2.
Row 5: Purl.
Row 6: K3, p1, k3, p1, k3.
Row 7: Purl.
Rows 8 to 23: Rep rows 6 and 7, 8 times more.

Row 24: As row 4.
Beg with a p row, work 3 rows in st st.
Cast off.

Top Section (make 6 pieces)
Using the thumb method and A, cast on 15 sts, WS facing to beg.
Beg with a p row, work 19 rows in st st.
Cast off.

Clock Face
Using the thumb method and B, cast on 36 sts.
Row 1 (RS): Purl.
Change to C and p 1 row.
Row 3: (K2tog, k2) to end (27 sts).
Row 4 and foll alt row: Purl.
Row 5: (K2tog, k1) to end (18 sts).
Row 7: (K2tog) to end (9 sts).
Thread yarn through sts on needle, pull tight and secure by threading yarn a second time through sts.

Making up

Note: Sew up clock using mattress stitch on right side, one stitch in from edge.

Base
Sew 5 pieces of base of clock together, making a box shape. Stuff base and sew 6th piece to complete the cube.

Middle Section
Sew up row ends of 4 pieces of middle section of clock. Stuff middle section, leaving top and bottom open. Sew lower edge to base all the way round.

Top Section
Make up as base of clock and sew top section to top of clock.

Clock Face
Sew outside edge of face of clock to front of top section all the way round. Embroider four short lines for numbers on face of clock in black and a long line from centre to 'twelve' and a shorter line to 'one': the clock will read one o'clock (see page 139 for how to begin and fasten off the embroidery invisibly).

How to make Mouse

Body and Head

Beg at back using the thumb method and D, cast on 5 sts.

Row 1 (WS): Purl.

Row 2: K1, (m1, k1) to end (9 sts).

Rows 3 and 4: Rep first 2 rows once (17 sts).

Beg with a purl row, work 7 rows in st st.

Row 12: K3, (k2tog, k1) 4 times, k2 (13 sts).

Beg with a purl row, work 3 rows in st st.

Row 16: K1, (k2tog, k1) to end (9 sts).

Row 17: Purl.

Row 18: (K2tog) twice, k1, k2tog, k2tog tbl (5 sts).

Thread yarn through sts on needle, pull tight and secure by threading yarn a second time through sts.

Ears (make 2)

Using the thumb method and D, cast on 6 sts.

Thread yarn through sts on needle, pull tight and secure by threading yarn a second time through sts.

Making up

Tail

Make a twisted cord out of 2 lengths of yarn E, each 50cm (20in) long (see page 139). Tie a tight knot 2¼in (6cm) from folded end and trim ends beyond knot.

Body and Head

Gather round cast-on stitches and enclose knotted end of tail in centre, pull tight and secure and sew through knot on wrong side to secure. Sew up row ends of body and head on right side, leaving a gap. Stuff body and head, pushing a tiny ball of stuffing into nose with tweezers or tip of scissors and sew up gap.

Ears

Sew up row ends of cast-on edge of ears. Sew ears to mouse on top of head with two clear knitted stitches in between.

Features

Embroider eyes in black, taking a tiny straight stitch. Embroider nose in pink, taking two horizontal stitches close together (see page 139 for how to begin and fasten off the embroidery invisibly).

LITTLE BO PEEP

Information you'll need

Finished size
Bo Peep measures 9in (23cm) high
Sheep measure 4½in (11.5cm) high

Materials
Any DK (US: light worsted) yarn
Note: Amounts are approximate
5g green (A)
10g pale pink (B)
25g white (C)
15g mauve (D)
10g brown (E)
5g beige (F)
25g golden cream (G)
Oddments of black, red and pale
pink for embroidery

1 pair of 3.25mm (UK10:US3) needles
and a spare needle the same size
Knitters' blunt-ended pins and a needle
for sewing up
Tweezers for stuffing small parts (optional)
Acrylic toy stuffing
Drinking straw
2 pipe cleaners
Red pencil for shading cheeks

Tension
26 sts x 34 rows to 4in (10cm) square over
st st using 3.25mm needles and DK yarn
before stuffing.

How to make Bo Peep

Shoes, Legs, Body and Head

Make Shoes, Legs and Body as Jack on page 34 from beg to **, using A for shoes and C for lower body.

Change to D for upper body and work 10 rows in st st.

Work Neck and Head as Dame on page 44 from ** to end.

Skirt of Dress

Beg at lower edge using the thumb method and C, cast on 54 sts.

P 1 row then k 1 row (this part is turned under).

Picot row (WS): K2, (yf, k2tog) to end.
Beg with a k row, work 2 rows in st st.
Work 2 rows in garter st.
Change to D and beg with a k row, work 20 rows in st st.

Row 28: (K2tog, k4) to end (45 sts).
Beg with a p row, work 3 rows in st st.
Change to A and dec:

Row 32: (K2tog, k3) to end (36 sts).
K 1 row then p 1 row.
Cast off k-wise.

Sleeves, Arms and Hands (make 2)

Make Sleeves, Arms and Hands as Dame on pages 44–5, using D for sleeve.

Sleeve Frills (make 2)

Using the thumb method and C, cast on 20 sts.

P 1 row then k 1 row (this part is turned under).

Picot row (WS): K2, (yf, k2tog) to end.
Beg with a k row, work 3 rows in st st, ending with a k row.
Cast off k-wise.

Neck Band

Make Neck Band as Dame on page 45, using D.

Hair

Make Hair as Jack on page 35, using E.

Bun and Hair Loops
Make Bun and Hair Loops as Dame on page 45, using E.

Hair Flowers
Make Hair Flowers as Dame on page 45, using A.

Crook
Using the thumb method and F, cast on 5 sts and work in rev st st, RS facing to beg. Beg with a p row, rev st st for 7½in (19cm).
Cast off.

Making up
Shoes, Legs, Body and Head
Sew up row ends of shoes and with markers at tips of toes, oversew cast-on stitches; leg seam will be ¼in (6mm) on inside edge of heel. Sew up ankles and place a ball of stuffing into toes. Sew up row ends of legs and sew round crotch. Stuff legs and sew up body seam. Stuff body and sew up row ends of head to halfway up head. Stuff head, pulling stitches on a thread tight at top of head and sew up remainder of row ends. To shape neck, take a double length of yarn B and sew a running stitch round row with marker at neck, sewing in and out of every half stitch. Pull tight and knot yarn, sewing ends into neck.

Skirt of Dress
Make up Skirt of Dress as Miss Muffet on page 86.

Sleeves, Arms and Hands
Make up Sleeves, Arms and Hands as Dame on page 46.

Sleeve Frills
Make up Sleeve Frills as Miss Muffet on page 86.

Neck Band
Make up Neck Band as Dame on page 46.

Features
Embroider Features as Jack on page 36.

Hair
Make up Hair as Jack on page 36.

Bun
Make up Bun as Dame on page 46.

Hair Loops and Flowers
Make up Hair Loops and Flowers as Dame on page 46.

Crook
Cut drinking straw to 5in (13cm). Take two pipe cleaners together and fold them in half. Push folded pipe cleaners into top of straw with 2in (5cm) of pipe cleaner showing at top. Sew up row ends of stick around straw and gather round stitches at top and bottom, pull tight and secure. Using picture as a guide, bend top of crook to shape and sew crook to hand of doll.

How to make Sheep
Make Sheep as Black Sheep on pages 47–8, using G for Body, C for Legs, beg with G for Head and change to C for face, C for Ears and G for Tail.

HEY DIDDLE DIDDLE

Information you'll need

Finished size
Cat and Fiddle measure 4in (10cm) high
Cow and Moon measure 18in (46cm) high
Little dog measures 3in (7½cm) high
Dish and spoon measure 4½in
(11½cm) high

Materials
Any DK (US: light worsted) yarn
Note: Amounts are approximate
20g white (A)
5g black (B)
5g brown (C)
5g honey (D)
10g pale brown (E)
5g biscuit (F)
10g lemon (G)
10g deep brown (H)
5g rust (I)
5g blue (J)
10g silver grey (K)
Oddments of black and green
for embroidery

1 pair of 3.25mm (UK10:US3) needles
Knitters' blunt-ended pins and a needle
for sewing up
Tweezers for stuffing small parts (optional)
Acrylic toy stuffing
Pipe cleaner

Tension
26 sts x 34 rows to 4in (10cm) square over
st st using 3.25mm needles and DK yarn
before stuffing.

Special abbreviation
M1: Pick up the horizontal loop between
the needles from front to back and work
into the back of it.

How to make Cat and Fiddle

Body

Using the thumb method and A, cast on 8 sts.

Row 1 and foll 2 alt rows: Purl.
Row 2 (RS): (Kfb) to end (16 sts).
Row 4: (Kfb, k1) to end (24 sts).
Row 6: (Kfb, k2) to end (32 sts).
Beg with a p row work 3 rows in st st.
Join on B and work in st st in stripe, carrying yarn loosely up side of work.
Using B, work 2 rows in st st.
Using A, work 4 rows in st st.
Using B, work 2 rows in st st.
Using A, work 2 rows in st st.

Row 20: Using A, (K2tog, k2) to end (24 sts).
Using A, p 1 row.
Using B, work 2 rows in st st.
Using A, work 2 rows in st st.
Row 26: Using A, (k2tog, k1) to end (16 sts).
Using A, cast off p-wise.

Head

Beg at centre back using the thumb method and A, cast on 8 sts.

Row 1 and foll alt row: Purl.
Row 2 (RS): (Kfb) to end (16 sts).
Row 4: (Kfb, k1) to end (24 sts).
Beg with a p row, work 9 rows in st st.
Row 14: K5, (k2tog, k1) 5 times, k4 (19 sts).
Row 15: Purl.
Row 16: K4, (k2tog, k1) 4 times, k3 (15 sts).
Row 17: (P2tog, p1) to end (10 sts).
Row 18: (K2tog) to end (5 sts).
Thread yarn through sts on needle, pull tight and secure by threading yarn a second time through sts.

Ears (make 2)

Using the thumb method and B, cast on 8 sts.

Row 1 (WS): Purl.
Row 2: (K2tog) to end (4 sts).
Thread yarn through sts on needle, pull tight and secure by threading yarn a second time through sts.

Hind Legs (make 2)

Using the thumb method and B, cast on 8 sts.

Row 1 (WS): Purl.
Row 2: (Kfb) to end (16 sts).
Beg with a p row, work 5 rows in st st.
Row 8: (K2tog) to end (8 sts).
Thread yarn through sts on needle, pull tight and secure by threading yarn a second time through sts.

Forearms (make 2)

Using the thumb method and B, cast on 10 sts.
Beg with a p row, work 7 rows in st st.
Change to A.
Row 8 (RS): K1, m1, k2, (k2tog) twice, k2, m1, k1 (10 sts).
Beg with a p row, work 3 rows st st.
Row 12: K1, (k2tog, k1) to end (7 sts).
Thread yarn through sts on needle, pull tight and secure by threading yarn a second time through sts.

Tail

Using the thumb method and B, cast on
10 sts.
Beg with a p row, work 3 rows in st st.
Row 4 (RS): K2tog, k to end (9 sts).
Beg with a p row, work 3 rows in st st.
Row 8: As row 4 (8 sts).
Beg with a p row, work 3 rows in st st.
Change to A for tip of tail and beg with
a k row, work 4 rows in st st.
Thread yarn through sts on needle,
pull tight and secure by threading yarn
a second time through sts.

Fiddle

Using the thumb method and C, cast on
10 sts.
Row 1 (WS): Purl.
Row 2: (K2, m1, k1, m1, k2) twice
(14 sts).
Beg with a p row, work 7 rows in st st.
Row 10: K2, (k2tog) twice, k2, (k2tog)
twice, k2 (10 sts).
Row 11: P1, (p2tog, p1) to end (7 sts).
Beg with a k row, work 6 rows in st st.
Thread yarn through sts on needle,
pull tight and secure by threading yarn
a second time through sts.

Fingerboard

Using the thumb method and D, cast on
3 sts, WS facing to beg.
Beg with a p row, work 9 rows in st st.
Cast off.

Bow

Using the thumb method and D, cast on
4 sts, WS facing to beg.
Beg with a p row, work 19 rows in st st.
Thread yarn through sts on needle, pull
tight and secure by threading yarn
a second time through sts.

Making up

Body

Sew up row ends of body and stuff,
keeping base flat.

Head

Sew up row ends of head, leaving a gap.
Stuff head, pushing stuffing into nose
and sew up gap. Sew head to body.

Ears

Sew up row ends of ears and with this
seam at centre back, sew ears to head.

Features

Embroider eyes in green, taking a small
chain stitch (see page 139 for how to begin
and fasten off the embroidery invisibly).
Using picture as a guide, embroider nose
and mouth in black using straight stitches.
Embroider straight stitches in B for stripes,
three at top of head between ears and two
at sides, taking a double stitch.

Hind Legs

Gather round cast-on stitches of hind legs,
pull tight and secure. Sew up row ends
leaving a gap; stuff and sew up gap.
Place cat on a flat surface and assemble
hind legs and sew to body.

Tail

Roll tail up from shaped row ends to
straight row ends and sew in place.
To curve tail, sew a running stitch along
inside of curve and pull to curve and
fasten off. Sew tail to cat at back.

Forearms

Sew up row ends of forearms and stuff,
pushing stuffing in with tweezers or tip
of scissors. With the seam at centre of
inside edge, sew across cast-on stitches.

Fiddle and Fingerboard

Sew up narrow row ends of fiddle from
stitches pulled tight on a thread to
decrease stitches and stuff narrow part,
pushing stuffing in with tweezers or tip
of scissors. Sew up row ends of fiddle
and stuff and, with seam at centre of
underneath edge, sew across cast-on
stitches. Sew fingerboard to fiddle and,
using picture as a guide, embroider a
straight stitch at end of fingerboard.

Bow

Take a pipe cleaner and fold in half and
put folded end of pipe cleaner into stitches
pulled tight on a thread of bow. Sew up
row ends along bow, enclosing pipe cleaner
inside. Cut excess pipe cleaner and gather
round cast-on stitches, pull tight and
secure. Using picture as a guide, assemble
arms, fiddle and bow and sew in place.

How to make Cow and Moon

Body
Make Body as Cow on page 74, using A.

Legs (make 4)
Beg at top using the thumb method and A, cast on 19 sts.
Beg with a p row, work 13 rows in st st.
Change to E and beg with a k row, work 4 rows in st st.
Row 18 (RS): K1, (k2tog, k1) to end (13 sts).
Cast off p-wise.

Patch
Using the thumb method and E, cast on 10 sts and work in garter st.
Row 1 (RS): Kfb, k to last st, kfb (12 sts).
Rows 2 to 4: Rep row 1, 3 times more (18 sts).
Work 10 rows in garter st.
Cast on 4 sts at beg of next 2 rows (26 sts).
Row 17: Kfb, k to last st, kfb (28 sts).
Row 18: As row 17 (30 sts).
Work 10 rows in garter st.
Row 29: K2tog, k to last 2 sts, k2tog tbl (28 sts).
Rows 30 to 33: Rep row 29, 4 times more, ending with a RS row (20 sts).
Cast off in garter st.

Head
Make Head as Cow on page 74, beg in F and change to A.

Ears (make 2)
Make Ears as Cow on page 74, using A.

Moon (make 2 pieces)
Using the thumb method and G, cast on 36 sts.
Row 1 and foll 4 alt rows: Purl.
Row 2 (RS): K2tog, k6, m1, k4, m1, k12, m1, k4, m1, k6, k2tog tbl (38 sts).
Row 4: K2tog, k7, m1, k4, m1, k12, m1, k4, m1, k7, k2tog tbl (40 sts).
Row 6: K2tog, k8, m1, k4, m1, k12, m1, k4, m1, k8, k2tog tbl (42 sts).
Row 8: K2tog, k9, m1, k4, m1, k12, m1, k4, m1, k9, k2tog tbl (44 sts).
Row 10: K2tog, k10, m1, k4, m1, k12, m1, k4, m1, k10, k2tog tbl (46 sts).
Row 11: P2tog tbl, p to last 2 sts, p2tog (44 sts).
Row 12: K2tog, k to last 2 sts, k2tog tbl (42 sts).

Rows 13 and 14: Rep rows 11 and 12 once (38 sts).
Row 15: As row 11 (36 sts).
Cast off.

Moon Nose
Using the thumb method and G, cast on 14 sts.
Row 1 and foll 4 alt rows: Purl.
Row 2 (RS): K5, (k2tog) twice, k5 (12 sts).
Row 4: K4, (k2tog) twice, k4 (10 sts).
Row 6: K3, (k2tog) twice, k3 (8 sts).
Row 8: K2, (k2tog) twice, k2 (6 sts).
Row 10: K1, (k2tog) twice, k1 (4 sts).
Thread yarn through sts on needle, pull tight and secure by threading yarn a second time through sts.

Making up

Cord

Make a twisted cord out of 4 pieces of yarn G, each measuring 60in (150cm) long (see page 139). Tie a knot 12in (30cm) from folded end and trim ends beyond knot.

Cow's Tail

Make Tail as Cow on page 75, using A.

Body

Fold cast-on stitches and cast-off stitches in half and sew up. Partly stuff end of body to halfway. Thread a large needle with the folded end of cord and pass cord through centre of cow, through lower edge and up through back. Finish stuffing body and sew up row ends and sew on tail. With 2in (5cm) of cord showing at lower edge, sew cord to cow above and below body to secure.

Legs

Sew up row ends of legs and stuff. Sew legs to body at front and back.

Patch

Using picture as a guide, place patch on back of cow, threading cord through centre of patch and sew outside edge of patch to cow all the way round.

Head and Ears

Make up Head and Ears as Cow on page 75.

Features of Cow

Embroider Features as Cow on page 75.

Moon

Place two pieces of moon together, matching all edges and sew up outside edge, leaving a gap at top. Enclose knot of cord in top of moon and sew in place securely. Stuff moon and sew up gap.

Features of Moon

Fold cast-on stitches of nose in half and sew up. Stuff nose and sew row ends to moon. Embroider eyes in black, taking a small chain stitch and then a second one on top (see page 139 for how to begin and fasten off the embroidery invisibly). Using picture as a guide, embroider mouth in black using straight stitches.

How to make Little Dog

Make Little Dog as Dog on pages 116–17, using H for Body, Head, Front Legs, Hind Legs and I for Ears and beg in H for Tail and change to I for tip of tail.

How to make Dish and Spoon

Dish (make 2 pieces)

Using the thumb method and J, cast on 74 sts and beg in garter st.

Join on A and work 4 rows in garter st.

Row 5 (RS): Using J, k2, (k2tog, k2) to end (56 sts).

Using J, k 1 row.

Cont in A and beg with a k row, work 4 rows in st st.

Row 11: *(K2, k2tog) twice, k12, (k2tog, k2) twice, rep from * once (48 sts).

Row 12 and foll 3 alt rows: Purl.

Row 13: *(K2, k2tog) twice, k8, (k2tog, k2) twice, rep from * once (40 sts).

Row 15: *(K1, k2tog) twice, k8, (k2tog, k1) twice, rep from * once (32 sts).

Row 17: *(K1, k2tog) twice, k4, (k2tog, k1) twice, rep from * once (24 sts).

Row 19: (K2tog) to end (12 sts).

Thread yarn through sts on needle, pull tight and secure by threading yarn a second time through sts.

Spoon

Using the thumb method and K, cast on 30 sts.

Row 1 (WS): Purl.

Row 2: K10, turn.

Row 3: S1p, p5, turn.

Row 4: S1k, k to end.

Row 5: Purl.

Row 6: K12, turn.

Row 7: S1p, p9, turn.

Row 8: S1k, k to end.

Row 9: Purl.

Rows 10 to 13: Rep rows 6 to 9 once.

Rows 14 to 17: Rep rows 2 to 5 once.

Rows 18 to 33: Rep rows 2 to 17 once.

Cast off.

Arms and Legs (make 8)

Note: Make 2 arms and 2 legs in A for dish and 2 arms and 2 legs in K for spoon. Using the thumb method and colour for dish or spoon, cast on 10 sts.

Row 1 (WS): Purl.

Row 2: K4, (kfb) twice, k4 (12 sts).

Beg with a p row, work 3 rows in st st.

Row 6: K4, (k2tog) twice, k4 (10 sts).

Cast off p-wise.

Making up

Features for Dish

Using picture as a guide, embroider features in black on front of dish, taking two small chain stitches for eyes, and embroider nose and mouth using straight stitches.

Dish

Using piece of thick cardboard, draw round outside edge of dish and cut out shape. Draw a line ½in (1.5cm) inside shape and cut out card from centre. Place cardboard frame between back and front of dish and sew up cast-on stitches all the way round.

Spoon

Sew up cast-on and cast-off stitches of spoon. This seam will be at centre back. Stuff handle, pushing stuffing in with tweezers or tip of scissors. Gather round row ends at top and bottom, pull tight and secure.

Features for Spoon

Using picture as a guide, embroider features in black on bowl of spoon, taking two small chain stitches for eyes, and embroider nose and mouth using straight stitches (see page 139 for how to begin and fasten off the embroidery invisibly).

Arms and Legs

Sew up cast-on and cast-off stitches of arms and legs and stuff. Gather round row ends, pull tight and secure. Sew arms and legs to dish and spoon.

FIVE LITTLE DUCKS

Information you'll need

Finished size
Mother duck measures 6½in (16cm) high
Ducklings measure 3in (7.5cm) high

Materials
Any DK (US: light worsted) yarn
Note: Amounts are approximate
50g gold (A)
10g orange (B)
50g yellow (C)
Oddment of black for features
1 pair of 3.25mm (US3:UK10) needles
Knitters' blunt-ended pins and a needle
for sewing up
Tweezers for stuffing small parts (optional)
Acrylic toy stuffing

Tension
25 sts x 54 rows to 4in (10cm) square over
garter st using 3.25mm needles and DK
yarn before stuffing.

Special abbreviation
M1: Pick up the horizontal loop between
the needles from front to back and work
into the back of it.

How to make Mother Duck

Body and Tail (make 2 pieces)

Beg at lower edge using the thumb method and A, cast on 30 sts and work in garter st.

Row 1: Knit.
Row 2: (K1, m1) twice, k26, (m1, k1) twice (34 sts).
Row 3: Knit.
Row 4: K1, m1, k to last st, m1, k1 (36 sts).
Rows 5 to 14: Rep rows 3 and 4, 5 times more (46 sts).
Row 15: Knit.
Row 16: K1, m1, k to end (47 sts).
Rows 17 to 22: Rep rows 15 and 16, 3 times more (50 sts).
Place a marker on first and last st of last row.
Work 10 rows in garter st.
Row 33: K1, k2tog, k to end (49 sts).
Row 34: Knit.
Rows 35 to 44: Rep rows 33 and 34, 5 times more (44 sts).
Row 45: K1, (k2tog) twice, k to end (42 sts).
Row 46: Knit.
Row 47: K1, (k2tog) twice, k24, turn.
Row 48: S1k, k to end (40 sts).
Row 49: Cast off 28 sts at beg of row and k to end (12 sts).
Row 50: K2tog, k to end (11 sts).
Rows 51 to 53: Work 3 rows in garter st.
Rows 54 to 57: Rep rows 50 to 53 once (10 sts).
Rows 58: As row 50 (9 sts).
Row 59: K2tog, k5, k2tog tbl (7 sts).

Row 60: K2tog, k3, k2tog tbl (5 sts).
Thread yarn through sts on needle, pull tight and secure by threading yarn a second time through sts.

Gusset

Beg at one end and, using A, cast on 1 st and work in garter st.

Row 1: (K1, p1, k1) into front of first st (3 sts).
Rows 2 and 3: Knit.
Row 4: K1, m1, k1, m1, k1 (5 sts).
Row 5: Knit.
Row 6: K1, m1, k to last st, m1, k1 (7 sts).
Rows 7 to 20: Rep rows 5 and 6, 7 times more (21 sts).
Work 60 rows in garter st.
Row 81: K2tog, k to last 2 sts, k2tog tbl (19 sts).
Row 82: Knit.
Rows 83 to 98: Rep last 2 rows 8 times more (3 sts).
Row 99: K3tog tbl (1 st).
Fasten off.

Head

Beg at lower edge using the thumb method and A, cast on 32 sts and work in garter st.

Row 1 (RS): Knit.
Row 2: K1, (m1, k2) to last st, m1, k1 (48 sts).
Work 22 rows in garter st.
Row 25: (K2tog, k4) to end (40 sts).
Work 3 rows in garter st.
Row 29: (K2tog, k3) to end (32 sts).

Row 30 and foll 2 alt rows: Knit.
Row 31: (K2tog, k2) to end (24 sts).
Row 33: (K2tog, k1) to end (16 sts).
Row 35: (K2tog) to end (8 sts).
Thread yarn through sts on needle, pull tight and secure by threading yarn a second time through sts.

Beak

Using the thumb method and B, cast on 23 sts and work in st st.

Row 1 and foll 2 alt rows (WS): Purl.
Row 2: K8, k3tog, k1, k3tog, k8 (19 sts).
Row 4: K8, k3tog, k8 (17 sts).
Row 6: K3, k3tog, k5, k3tog, k3 (13 sts).
Beg with a p row, work 5 rows in st st.
Row 12: K2, k3tog, k3, k3tog, k2 (9 sts).
Row 13: Purl.
Row 14: K1, k3tog, k1, k3tog, k1 (5 sts).
Thread yarn through sts on needle, pull tight and secure by threading yarn a second time through sts.

Wings (make 2)

Using the thumb method and A, cast on 20 sts.

Row 1 and foll 3 alt rows: Purl.
Row 2 (RS): (K1, m1, k8, m1, k1) twice (24 sts).
Row 4: (K1, m1, k10, m1, k1) twice (28 sts).
Row 6: (K1, m1, k12, m1, k1) twice (32 sts).
Row 8: (K1, m1, k14, m1, k1) twice (36 sts).

Row 9: K12, p12, k12.

Row 10: (K1, m1, k16, m1, k1) twice (40 sts).

Row 11: Purl.

Row 12: K1, m1, k to last st, m1, k1 (42 sts).

Row 13: K13, p16, k13.

Row 14: As row 12 (44 sts).

Row 15: Purl.

Row 16: K1, m1, k18, k2tog tbl, k2, k2tog, k18, m1, k1 (44 sts).

Row 17: K14, p16, k14

Row 18: As row 16.

Row 19: Purl.

Row 20: As row 16.

Row 21: K15, p14, k15.

Rows 22 to 24: Rep rows 18 to 20.

Row 25: K16, p12, k16.

Row 26: As row 16.

Row 27: Purl.

Row 28: K1, m1, k16, k2tog, k2tog tbl, k2, (k2tog) twice, k16, m1, k1 (42 sts).

Row 29: K17, p8, k17.

Row 30: K1, m1, k15, k2tog, k2tog tbl, k2, (k2tog) twice, k15, m1, k1 (40 sts).

Row 31: P17, p2tog, p2, p2tog tbl, p17 (38 sts).

Row 32: K1, m1, k13, k2tog, k2tog tbl, k2, (k2tog) twice, k13, m1, k1 (36 sts). Cast off p-wise.

Making up

Body and Tail

Place two sides of body and tail together, matching all edges and sew around top edge from marker to marker. Turn right side out and stuff body and tail with plenty of stuffing.

Gusset

Sew tips of gusset, one to each marker. Sew side edges of gusset from marker to marker, leaving a gap. Place more stuffing into base and sew up gap.

Head

Sew up row ends of head and stuff. Pin and sew lower edge of head to duck, all the way round.

Beak

Sew up row ends of beak and stuff. Pin and sew cast-on stitches of beak to front of head.

Wings

Bringing row ends together, fold cast-on and cast-off stitches of wings in half and sew these edges together. Sew up row ends of wings; this will be the top edge. Pin and sew wings to each side of duck.

Features

Embroider eyes in black, marking their position on each side of head. Work a vertical chain stitch for each eye and then a second chain stitch on top of the first (see page 139 for how to begin and fasten off the embroidery invisibly).

How to make Ducklings

Body and Tail (make 2 pieces per duckling)

Beg at lower edge using the thumb method and C, cast on 10 sts and work in garter st.

Row 1: Knit.
Row 2: (K1, m1) twice, k6, (m1, k1) twice (14 sts).
Row 3: Knit.
Row 4: K1, m1, k to last st, m1, k1 (16 sts).
Rows 5 and 6: Rep rows 3 and 4 once (18 sts).
Row 7: Knit.
Row 8: K1, m1, k to end (19 sts).
Rows 9 and 10: Rep rows 7 and 8 once (20 sts).
Place a marker on first and last st of last row.
Work 4 rows in garter st.
Row 15: K1, k2tog, k to end (19 sts).
Row 16: Knit.
Row 17: K1, (k2tog) twice, k to end (17 sts).

Rows 18 and 19: Rep rows 16 and 17 once (15 sts).
Row 20: Knit.
Row 21: K1, (k2tog) twice, k3, turn.
Row 22: S1k, k to end (13 sts).
Row 23: Cast off 7 sts at beg of row and k to end (6 sts).
Row 24: K2tog, k to end (5 sts).
Work 4 rows in garter st.
Row 29: K2tog, k1, k2tog tbl (3 sts).
Row 30: K3tog tbl (1 st).
Fasten off.

Gusset (make 1 per duckling)

Using C, cast on 1 st and work in garter st.
Row 1: (K1, p1, k1) into front of first st (3 sts).
Work 2 rows in garter st.
Row 4: K1, m1, k1, m1, k1 (5 sts).
Row 5: Knit.
Row 6: K1, m1, k to last st, m1, k1 (7 sts).
Rows 7 and 8: Rep rows 5 and 6 once (9 sts).
Work 30 rows in garter st.

Row 39: K2tog, k to last 2 sts, k2tog tbl (7 sts).
Row 40: Knit.
Rows 41 to 44: Rep rows 39 and 40 twice (3 sts).
Row 45: K3tog tbl (1 st).
Fasten off.

Head (make 1 per duckling)

Using the thumb method and C, cast on 16 sts and work in garter st.
Row 1 (RS): Knit.
Row 2: K1, (m1, k2) to last st, m1, k1 (24 sts).
Work 8 rows in garter st.
Row 11: (K2tog, k2) to end (18 sts).
Work 3 rows in garter st.
Row 15: (K2tog, k1) to end (12 sts).
Row 16: Knit.
Row 17: (K2tog) to end (6 sts).
Thread yarn through sts on needle, pull tight and secure by threading yarn a second time through sts.

Beak (make 1 per duckling)

Using the thumb method and B, cast on 9 sts and work in st st.
Row 1 (WS): Purl.
Row 2: K2, k2tog, k1, k2tog, k2 (7 sts).
Beg with a p row, work 3 rows in st st.
Thread yarn through sts on needle, pull tight and secure by threading yarn a second time through sts.

Wings (make 2 per duckling)

Using the thumb method and C, cast on 6 sts and work in garter st.
Row 1 (RS): Knit.
Row 2: (K1, m1, k1, m1, k1) twice (10 sts).

Row 3: Knit.
Row 4: (K1, m1, k3, m1, k1) twice (14 sts).
Row 5: Knit.
Row 6: K1, m1, k4, (k2tog) twice, k4, m1, k1 (14 sts).
Rows 7 and 8: Rep rows 5 and 6 once.
Row 9: K6, k2tog, k6 (13 sts).
Cast off in garter st.

Making up

Make up Body and Tail, Gusset, Head and Wings as Mother Duck. Make up beak as Mother Duck, pushing stuffing in with tweezers or tip of scissors. Embroider eyes in black, taking just one chain stitch, as Mother Duck.

OLD MOTHER HUBBARD

Information you'll need

Finished size
Mother Hubbard measures 9in
(23cm) high
Dog measures 3in (8cm) high

Materials
Any DK (US: light worsted) yarn
Note: Amounts are approximate
10g green (A)
10g pale pink (B)
20g white (C)
10g plum (D)
10g grey (E)
10g beige (F)
10g brown (G)
5g dark brown (H)
Oddments of black, red and pale
pink for embroidery

1 pair of 3.25mm (UK10:US3) needles
and a spare needle the same size
Knitters' blunt-ended pins and a needle
for sewing up
Tweezers for stuffing small parts (optional)
Acrylic toy stuffing
Red pencil for shading cheeks

Tension
26 sts x 34 rows to 4in (10cm) square over
st st using 3.25mm needles and DK yarn
before stuffing.

Special abbreviation
M1: Pick up the horizontal loop between
the needles from front to back and work
into the back of it.

How to make Mother Hubbard

Shoes, Legs, Body and Head

Make Shoes, Legs, Body and Head as Jack on page 34, using A for shoes, C for lower body and A for upper body.

Petticoat

Using the thumb method and C, cast on 54 sts.

Row 1 (RS): K2, (yf, k2tog) to end.

Row 2: Knit.

Beg with a k row, work 16 rows in st st.

Row 19: (K2tog, k4) to end (45 sts).

Beg with a p row, work 3 rows in st st.

Row 23: (K2tog, k3) to end (36 sts).

Cast off p-wise.

Skirt

Beg at lower edge using the thumb method and D, cast on 60 sts and beg in garter st.

Garter st 2 rows.

Join on A and beg with a k row work 22 rows in st st in stripe, 2 rows A then 2 rows D, and do this alternately carrying yarn loosely up side of work.

Cont in stripe and dec:

Row 25 (RS): (K2tog, k3) to end (48 sts).

Beg with a p row, work 3 rows in stripe.

Cont in D and dec:

Row 29: (K2tog, k2) to end (36 sts).

Work 2 rows in garter st, ending with a RS row.

Cast off in garter st.

Sleeves and Hands (make 2)

Make Sleeves and Hands as Jack on page 34, using A for sleeve.

Cuffs (make 2)

Make Cuffs as Jack on page 35, using A.

Hair

Make Hair as Jack on page 35, using E.

Shawl

Using the thumb method and F, cast on 49 sts.

Row 1 (WS): K1, (yf, k2tog) to last 2 sts, yf, k2tog tbl.

Row 2: K3tog, (yf, k2tog) to last 2 sts, yf, k2tog tbl (47 sts).

Rows 3 to 23: Rep row 2, 21 times more (5 sts).

Row 24: K3tog, yf, k2tog tbl (3 sts).

Row 25: K3tog tbl.

Fasten off.

Mob Cap

Crown piece

Using the thumb method and C, cast on 36 sts.

Row 1 (WS): Purl.

Row 2: K1, m1, (k2, m1) to last st, k1 (54 sts).

Beg with a p row, work 7 rows in st st.

Row 10: (K2tog, k4) to end (45 sts).

Row 11 and foll 3 alt rows: Purl.

Row 12: (K2tog, k3) to end (36 sts).

Row 14: (K2tog, k2) to end (27 sts).

Row 16: (K2tog, k1) to end (18 sts).

Row 18: (K2tog) to end (9 sts).

Thread yarn through sts on needle, pull tight and secure by threading yarn a second time through sts.

Cap Frill

Using the thumb method and C, cast on 100 sts and work in garter st.
Work 4 rows in garter st.
Row 5 (RS): (K2tog) to end (50 sts).
Cast off in garter st.

Making up

Shoes, Legs, Body and Head

Make up Shoes, Legs, Body and Head as Jack on page 36.

Petticoat

Sew up row ends of petticoat and place on doll. Sew cast-off stitches at waist to last row of lower body all the way round.

Skirt

Sew up row ends of skirt and place on doll. Sew cast-off stitches of skirt to first row of upper body all the way round.

Sleeves, Hands and Cuffs

Make up Sleeves, Hands and Cuffs as Jack on page 36.

Features

Embroider Features as Jack on page 36.

Hair

Make up Hair as Jack on page 36.

Shawl

Place shawl around shoulders of doll and sew in place.

Mob Cap

Join row ends of crown piece of mob cap and stuff top lightly. Sew lower edge of crown piece to head all the way round. Place cap frill around head and sew up row ends and sew cast-off stitches of frill to cast-on stitches of crown piece.

old mother hubbard

How to make Dog

Body

Using the thumb method and G, cast on 7 sts.

Row 1 (WS): Purl.

Row 2: K1, (m1, k1) to end (13 sts).

Rep first 2 rows once (25 sts).

Beg with a p row, work 15 rows in st st.

Row 20: (K2tog, k3) to end (20 sts).

Row 21: Purl.

Row 22: (K2tog, k2) to end (15 sts).

Row 23: Purl.

Cast off.

Head

Using the thumb method and G, cast on 10 sts.

Row 1 and foll alt row: Purl.

Row 2 (RS): K1, (m1, k1) to end (19 sts).

Row 4: K5, (m1, k3) 4 times, k2 (23 sts).

Beg with a p row, work 5 rows in st st.

Row 10: K3, (k2tog, k1) 6 times, k2 (17 sts).

Row 11: P3, (p2tog, p1) 4 times, p2 (13 sts).

Row 12: (K1 tbl) to end.

Beg with a p row, work 3 rows in st st.

Row 16: K1, (k2tog, k1) to end (9 sts).

Thread yarn through sts on needle, pull tight and secure by threading yarn a second time through sts.

Front Legs (make 2)

Beg at paw using the thumb and method G, cast on 10 sts.

Beg with a p row, work 3 rows in st st.

Row 4 (RS): K2, (k2tog, k2) twice (8 sts).

Row 5: Purl.

Row 6: K1, m1, k6, m1, k1 (10 sts).

Beg with a p row, work 3 rows in st st.

Place a marker on first and last st of last row.

Row 10: K2tog, k to last 2 sts, k2tog tbl (8 sts).

Row 11: Purl.

Rows 12 and 13: Rep rows 10 and 11 once (6 sts).

Row 14: As row 10 (4 sts).

Cast off p-wise.

Hind Legs (make 2)

Using the thumb method and G, cast on 8 sts.

Beg with a p row, work 3 rows in st st.

Row 4 (RS): K3, m1, k2, m1, k3 (10 sts).

Row 5: Purl.

Row 6: K4, m1, k2, m1, k4 (12 sts).

Beg with a p row, work 3 rows in st st.

Row 10: (K2tog, k1) to end (8 sts).
Row 11: Purl.
Row 12: (K2tog) to end (4 sts).
Thread yarn through sts on needle, pull tight and secure by threading yarn a second time through sts.

Ears (make 2)
Using the thumb method and H, cast on 3 sts.
Row 1 and foll 2 alt rows: Purl.
Row 2 (RS): K1, (m1, k1) twice (5 sts).
Row 4: K1, m1, k to last st, m1, k1 (7 sts).
Row 6: As row 4 (9 sts).
Row 7: Purl.
Cast off.

Tail
Using the thumb method and G, cast on 10 sts.
Beg with a p row, work 3 rows in st st.
Row 4 (RS): K2tog, k to end (9 sts).
Beg with a p row, work 3 rows in st st.
Row 8: As row 4 (8 sts).
Beg with a p row, work 3 rows in st st.
Change to H for tip of tail and beg with a k row, work 4 rows in st st.
Thread yarn through sts on needle, pull tight and secure by threading yarn a second time through sts.

Making up
Body
Gather round cast-on stitches of body, pull tight and secure and sew up row ends. Stuff body, leaving cast-off stitches at neck open.

Head
Gather round cast-on stitches of head and sew up row ends leaving a gap. Stuff head, pushing a tiny ball of stuffing into snout with tweezers or tip of scissors and sew up gap.

Front Legs
Gather round cast-on stitches of legs, pull tight and secure. Sew up row ends of legs from paws to markers. Stuff legs, pushing stuffing in with tweezers or tip of scissors. Sew legs to body. Sew head to body.

Hind Legs
Gather round cast-on stitches, pull tight and secure and sew up row ends of hind legs leaving a gap. Stuff and sew up gap. Position hind legs and sew to sides of body.

Ears
Join row ends of ears and, with this seam at centre of inside edge, sew ears to head at each side. Sew lower edge of ears in place.

Tail
Roll tail up from shaped row ends to straight row ends and sew in place. To curve tail, sew a running stitch along inside of curve and pull to curve and fasten off. Sew tail to dog at back.

Features
Embroider eyes in black, taking a small chain stitch for each eye. Using picture as a guide, embroider nose and mouth using straight stitches (see page 139 for how to begin and fasten off the embroidery invisibly).

old mother hubbard

117

ONE, TWO, THREE, FOUR, FIVE

Information you'll need

Finished size
Doll measures 6½in (16.5cm) high
Fish measures 2in (5cm) long

Materials
Any DK (US: light worsted) yarn
Note: Amounts are approximate
5g red (A)
5g pale pink (B)
5g white (C)
5g orange (D)
10g gold (E)
5g brown (F)
5g blue (G)
5g lemon (H)
5g oatmeal (I)
5g mid brown (J)
Oddments of black and red
for embroidery

1 pair of 3.25mm (US3:UK10) needles and
a spare needle of the same size
4mm (US6:UK8) needle
Knitters' blunt-ended pins and a needle
for sewing up
Tweezers for stuffing small parts (optional)
Acrylic toy stuffing
Pipe cleaner
Plastic drinking straw
Red pencil for shading cheeks

Tension
26 sts x 34 rows to 4in (10cm) square over
st st using 3.25mm needles and DK yarn
before stuffing.

Special abbreviation
M1: Pick up the horizontal loop between
the needles from front to back and work
into the back of it.

How to make Doll

Body and Head
Make Body and Head as Girls and Boys on page 130, using C for lower body and D for upper body.

Boots and Legs
Beg at sole of boot using the thumb method and A, cast on 10 sts.
Row 1 (WS): Purl.
Row 2: K2, (m1, k2) to end (14 sts).
Beg with a p row, work 3 rows in st st.
Shape boot
Row 6: K5, (k2tog) twice, k5 (12 sts).
Row 7: P3, p2tog, p2, p2tog, p3 (10 sts).
Work 4 rows in st st.
Work 2 rows in garter st.
Change to B for leg and beg with a k row, work 10 rows in st st.
Cast off.

Shorts
First leg
Beg at lower edge using the thumb method and E, cast on 16 sts.
Row 1 (RS): Purl.
Beg with a p row, work 5 rows in st st.
Cast off 1 st at beg of next 2 rows (14 sts).
Break yarn and set aside.
Second leg
Work as first leg but do not break yarn.
Join legs
With RS facing, k across sts of second leg and then with the same yarn, cont knitting across sts of first leg (28 sts).
Beg with a p row, work 5 rows in st st.
Cast off.

Coat
Using the thumb method and E, cast on 30 sts and beg in garter st.
Work 2 rows in garter st.
Beg with a k row, work 16 rows in st st and k the first 2 and last 2 sts on every p row.
Row 19 (RS): K2tog, * k1, (k2tog) twice, rep from * 4 times, k1, k2tog (18 sts).
Work 2 rows in garter st.
Row 22: K1, (m1, k2) to last st, m1, k1 (27 sts).
Work 2 rows in garter st.
Cast off in garter st.

Sleeves and Hands (make 2)
Make Sleeves and Hands as Little Boy on page 50, using E for sleeves.

Cuffs (make 2)
Make Cuffs as Little Boy on page 50, using E.

Hair
Make Hair as Girls and Boys on page 130, using F.

Hat
Beg at lower edge using the thumb method and E, cast on 42 sts and beg in garter st.
Work 4 rows in garter st.
Row 5 (WS): P2, (p2tog, p2) to end (32 sts).
Beg with a k row, work 8 rows in st st.
Row 14: (K2tog, k2) to end (24 sts).
Row 15 and foll alt row: Purl.
Row 16: (K2tog, k1) to end (16 sts).
Row 18: (K2tog) to end (8 sts).
Thread yarn through sts on needle, pull tight and secure by threading yarn a second time through sts.

Making up

Body and Head

Make up Body and Head as Girls and Boys on page 131.

Boots and Legs

Fold cast-on stitches of boots in half and sew up. Sew up row ends of boots and place a ball of stuffing into toe of each boot, pushing stuffing in with tweezers or tip of scissors. Sew up row ends of legs and stuff, pushing stuffing in with tweezers or tip of scissors. With toes pointing forwards, sew cast-off stitches of legs to lower edge of body.

Shorts

Sew up leg seams of shorts from lower edge to crotch. Sew round crotch and sew up row ends at centre back. Place shorts on doll and sew cast-off stitches to first row of upper body all the way round.

Coat

Place coat around doll and sew coat to neck beneath collar.

Sleeves and Hands

Join row ends of hands and place a small ball of stuffing into hands, pushing stuffing in with tweezers or tip of scissors. Sew up sleeves from wrists to markers at underarm. Stuff arms, leaving armholes open. Sew arms to doll beneath collar at either side, sewing through coat to body.

Cuffs

Make up Cuffs as Little Boy on page 51.

Features

Embroider Features as Girls and Boys on page 131.

Hair

Make up Hair as Girls and Boys on page 131.

Hat

Sew up row ends of hat and place on head. Sew hat to head above brim all the way round and turn brim up at front.

one, two, three, four, five

How to make Fish and Net

Fish

Using the thumb method and G, cast on
6 sts.

Row 1 and foll alt row (WS): Purl.

Row 2: K1, (m1, k1) to end (11 sts).

Row 4: K1, m1, k4, m1, k1, m1, k4, m1,
k1 (15 sts).

Join on H and p 2 rows.

Using G, p 1 row then k 1 row.

Using H, p 2 rows.

Cont in G and p 1 row then k 1 row.

Row 13: P1, * p2tog, p2, k2tog, p1,
rep from * once (11 sts).

Row 14: K1, (k2tog) twice, k1, (k2tog)
twice, k1 (7 sts).

Row 15: P2, m1, p3, m1, p2 (9 sts).

Work 2 rows in st st.

Row 18: K1, (m1, k1) to end (17 sts).

Cast off p-wise.

Fins (make 2)

Using the thumb method and G, cast on
5 sts, RS facing to beg.

Cast off p-wise.

Rim of Net

Using the thumb method and J, cast on
28 sts, WS facing to beg.

Beg with a p row, work 3 rows in st st.

Cast off.

Pole

Using the thumb method and J, cast on
5 sts, WS facing to beg.

Beg with a p row, work in st st for 3½in
(9cm).

Cast off.

Net

Using the thumb method and I, cast on
11 sts.

Row 1 (WS): K1, *(yrn) twice, k2tog,
rep from * 4 times.

Row 2: K next row dropping extra loops.

Rows 3 to 14: Rep rows 1 and 2,
6 times more.

Cast off very loosely using the
4mm needle.

Making up

Fish and Fins
Sew up row ends of fish, pushing in a little stuffing with tweezers or tip of scissors. Gather row ends of one end of fin and pull tight and secure. Sew each fin to either side of fish.

Features
Embroider an eye in black on each side of fish, taking a tiny stitch (see page 139 for how to begin and fasten off the embroidery invisibly).

Rim of Net, Pole and Net
Place a pipe cleaner along wrong side of rim of net and sew up cast-on and cast-off stitches along piece, enclosing pipe cleaner inside. The pipe cleaner will be sticking out of both ends. Cut drinking straw to 3in (8cm). Bring ends of pipe cleaner together and insert into one end of drinking straw as far as knitting. Sew up row ends of pole around drinking straw and sew pole to rim of net where they meet. Gather round end of pole, pull tight and secure.

Fold net, bringing two opposite corners of net together to make a triangle and sew up one side. Sew upper edge of net to lower edge of rim of net.

one, two, three, four, five

FIVE LITTLE MONKEYS

Information you'll need

Finished size
Monkeys measure 4in (10cm) high
Bed measures 9in (23cm) long

Materials
Any DK (US: light worsted) yarn
Note: Amounts are approximate)
20g brown (A)
10g beige (B)
20g white (C)
40g pale brown (D)
30g red (E)
20g burnt orange (F)
Oddment of black for features
1 pair of 3.25mm (UK10:US3) needles
Knitters' blunt-ended pins and a needle
for sewing up
Acrylic toy stuffing
25 pipe cleaners
Small piece of wadding (optional)

Tension
26 sts x 34 rows to 4in (10cm) square over
st st using 3.25mm needles and DK yarn
before stuffing.

Special abbreviation
M1: Pick up the horizontal loop between
the needles from front to back and work
into the back of it.

How to make Monkey

Body and Head

Beg at base using the thumb method and A, cast on 10 sts.

Row 1 (WS): Purl.

Row 2: K2, (m1, k2) to end (14 sts).

Rows 3 and 4: Rep rows 1 and 2 once (20 sts).

Row 5: Purl.

Row 6: K4, (m1, k4) to end (24 sts).

Beg with a p row, work 7 rows in st st.

Row 14: (K2tog, k2) to end (18 sts).

Row 15 and foll alt row: Purl.

Row 16: (K2tog, k1) to end (12 sts).

Row 18: (K2, m1) twice, k4, (m1, k2) twice (16 sts).

Beg with a p row, work 9 rows in st st.

Row 28: (K2tog) to end (8 sts).

Thread yarn through sts on needle, pull tight and secure by threading yarn a second time through sts.

Eye Piece

Using the thumb method and B, cast on 8 sts.

Row 1 (WS): Purl.

Thread yarn through sts on needle, pull tight and secure by threading yarn a second time through sts.

Muzzle

Using the thumb method and B, cast on 10 sts.

Row 1 (WS): Purl.

Row 2: (K1, k3tog, k1) twice (6 sts).

Thread yarn through sts on needle, pull tight and secure by threading yarn a second time through sts.

Ears (make 2)

Using the thumb method and B, cast on 5 sts.

Thread yarn through sts on needle, pull tight and secure by threading yarn a second time through sts.

Arms and Legs (make 4)

Using the thumb method and A, cast on 8 sts, WS facing for first row.

Beg with a p row, work 9 rows in st st.

Change to B and work 4 rows in st st.

Thread yarn through sts on needle, pull tight and secure by threading yarn a second time through sts.

Tail

Using the thumb method and A, cast on 6 sts, WS facing for first row.

Beg with a p row, work 21 rows in st st.

Thread yarn through sts on needle, pull tight and secure by threading yarn a second time through sts.

Making up

Body and Head

Sew up row ends of head and body to halfway down body. Stuff head and body. Finish sewing up row ends of body and gather round cast-on stitches, pull tight and secure.

Eyepiece and Muzzle

Sew up row ends of muzzle and place a tiny ball of stuffing inside. Sew eyepiece to head and sew muzzle to lower edge of eyepiece and head all the way round.

Features

Embroider eyes in black, taking a small chain stitch. Using picture as a guide, embroider nose and mouth in black using straight stitches (see page 139 for how to begin and fasten off the embroidery invisibly).

Ears

Sew ears to head at each side.

Arms and Legs

Take 4 pipe cleaners and fold each one in half. For each arm and leg, place folded end of pipe cleaner into wrong side of stitches pulled tight on a thread. Sew up row ends using mattress stitch around pipe cleaner. Trim excess pipe cleaner and sew arms and legs to monkey. Bend at knees and elbows.

Tail

Fold pipe cleaner in half and place folded end of pipe cleaner into wrong side of stitches pulled tight on a thread. Sew up row ends using mattress stitch around pipe cleaner. Trim excess pipe cleaner and sew tail to monkey at back. Bend tail.

How to make Bed

Base and Mattress

Using the thumb method and C, cast on 30 sts, RS facing to beg.
Beg with a k row, work 60 rows in st st.
Work 2 rows in garter st.
Change to D and beg with a k row, work 14 rows in st st.
Work 2 rows in garter st.
Cont in st st and cast on 12 sts at beg of next 2 rows (54 sts).
Beg with a k row, work 58 rows in st st.
Cast off 12 sts k-wise at beg of next row (42 sts).
Cast off 12 sts p-wise at beg of next row and k to end (30 sts).
Beg with a k row, work 14 rows in st st.
Cast off k-wise.

Bed Head and Foot
(make 2 pieces)

Note: Foll individual instructions for Bed Head and Bed Foot.
Beg at lower edge using the thumb method and D, cast on 34 sts.

Row 1 (WS): Purl.
Work 2 rows in garter st.
Beg with a k row, work 14 rows in st st.
Work 2 rows in garter st.
For bed head
Beg with a k row, work 50 rows in st st.
Cast off.
For bed foot
Beg with a k row, work 28 rows in st st.
Cast off.

Eiderdown (make 2 pieces)

Using the thumb method and E, cast on 40 sts.
Row 1 (WS): Purl.
Join on F and work 56 rows in st st in stripe, carrying yarn loosely up side of work and beg with a k row, work 2 rows F then 2 rows F and do this alternately, finishing with 2 rows E.
Cast off in E.

Pillows (make 2)

Using the thumb method and E, cast on 20 sts, WS facing to beg.
Beg with a p row, work 35 rows in st st.
Cast off.

Making up
Base and mattress

Sew up corners of base and stuff. Sew mattress to base all the way round.

Head and Foot

Sew up cast-on and cast-off stitches of bed head and foot and stuff lightly, keeping work flat. Using mattress stitch, sew up row ends at sides. Sew bed head and foot to ends of bed, sewing garter-st rows of head and foot to garter-st rows of bed.

Eiderdown

Cut piece of wadding, if using, to size of eiderdown and place between eiderdown pieces. Sew up row ends and top edge of eiderdown. If not using wadding, stuff eiderdown very lightly, keeping flat. Sew up lower edge and place eiderdown on bed.

Pillows

Sew up cast-on and cast-off stitches of pillows and sew up row ends of one end. Stuff pillow and sew up remaining row ends.

GIRLS AND BOYS COME OUT TO PLAY

Information you'll need

Finished size

Boys and Girls measure 6½in
(16.5cm) high

Materials

Any DK (US: light worsted) yarn

Note: Amounts are approximate)
Make a selection of dolls choosing
their clothes and colours as desired.

For one doll:

5g colour for shoes (A)
5g white (B)
5g pale pink (C)
5g colour for upper body and sleeves (D)
5g colour for dungarees or pinafore (E)
5g colour for hair (F)
Oddments of black and red for features

1 pair of 3.25mm (US3:UK10) needles and
a spare needle of the same size
Knitters' blunt-ended pins and a needle
for sewing up
Tweezers for stuffing small parts (optional)
Acrylic toy stuffing
Red pencil for shading cheeks

Tension

26 sts x 34 rows to 4in (10cm) square over
st st using 3.25mm needles and DK yarn
before stuffing.

Special abbreviation

M1: Pick up the horizontal loop between
the needles from front to back and work
into the back of it.

How to make Doll

Body and Head

Beg at lower edge using the thumb method and B for lower body, cast on 24 sts.
Place a marker at centre of cast-on sts.
Beg with a p row, work 5 rows in st st.
Change to D for upper body and beg with a k row, work 12 rows in st st.
Change to C for head and work 2 rows in st st.

Row 20 (RS): K3, m1, (k6, m1) 3 times k3 (28 sts).

Beg with a p row, work 7 rows in st st.

Row 28: (K2tog, k2) to end (21 sts).

Row 29 and foll alt row: Purl.

Row 30: (K2tog, k1) to end (14 sts).

Row 32: (K2tog) to end (7 sts).

Thread yarn through sts on needle, pull tight and secure by threading yarn a second time through sts.

Shoes, Socks and Legs (make 2)

Beg at sole of shoe using the thumb method and A, cast on 10 sts.

Row 1 (WS): Purl.

Row 2: K2, (m1, k2) to end (14 sts).

Beg with a p row, work 3 rows in st st.

Shape shoe

Row 6: K5, (k2tog) twice, k5 (12 sts).

Change to B for sock and dec:

Row 7: P3, p2tog, p2, p2tog, p3 (10 sts).

Work 2 rows in garter st.

Change to C for leg and beg with a k row, work 14 rows in st st.

Cast off.

Short Sleeves, Arms and Hands (make 2)

Beg at shoulder using the thumb method and D, cast on 4 sts.

Row 1 (WS): Purl.

Row 2: K1, m1, k to last st, m1, k1 (6 sts).

Rows 3 to 6: Rep rows 1 and 2 twice more (10 sts).

Row 7: Knit.

Change to C for arm and beg with a k row, work 8 rows in st st.

Row 16: K2, (k2tog, k2) twice (8 sts).

Beg with a p row, work 4 rows in st st, ending with a k row.

Thread yarn through sts on needle, pull tight and secure by threading yarn a second time through sts.

Hair

Beg at lower edge using the thumb method and F, cast on 28 sts and work in garter st.

Work 12 rows in garter st.

Row 13 (RS): (K2tog, k2) to end (21 sts).

Row 14 and foll alt row: Knit.

Row 15: (K2tog, k1) to end (14 sts).

Row 17: (K2tog) to end (7 sts).

Thread yarn through sts on needle, pull tight and secure by threading yarn a second time through sts.

Dungarees

Note: Foll instructions for short-leg or for long-leg dungarees.

First leg

Beg at lower edge using the thumb method and E, cast on 16 sts.

Row 1 (RS): Purl.

Beg with a p row, work 5 rows in st st for short leg or 15 rows in st st for long leg.

Cast off 1 st at beg of next 2 rows (14 sts). Break yarn and set aside.

Second leg

Work as first leg but do not break yarn.

Join legs

With RS facing, k across sts of second leg and then with the same yarn, cont knitting across sts of first leg (28 sts).

Beg with a p row, work 5 rows in st st.

**Shape back

Cast off 10 sts p-wise, p7 (8 sts now on RH needle), cast off 10 sts p-wise (8 sts).

Fasten off and rejoin yarn to rem sts.

Work bib

Next row: K1, p to last st, k1.

Next row: Knit.
Rep last 2 rows 3 times more.
Cast off k-wise.

Straps (make 2)
Using the thumb method and E, cast on 18 sts, RS facing to beg.
Cast off p-wise.

Pinafore
Using the thumb method and E, cast on 42 sts, and beg in garter st, RS facing to beg.
Work 2 rows in garter st.
Beg with a k row, work 13 rows in st st, ending on a k row.
Row 16: (P2tog, p1) to end (28 sts).
Work as dungarees from ** to end.

Straps (make 2)
Make Straps as Dungarees in E.

Making up
Body and Head
Sew up row ends of body and head and stuff. Bring seam and marker together at lower edge and sew up cast-on stitches. To shape neck, take a double length of yarn to match body and sew a running stitch round last row of body, sewing in and out of every half stitch. Pull tight and knot yarn, sewing ends into neck.

Shoes, Socks and Legs
Fold cast-on stitches of shoes in half and sew up. Sew up row ends of shoes and socks and place a ball of stuffing into toes, pushing stuffing in with tweezers or tip of scissors. Sew up row ends of legs and stuff, pushing stuffing in with tweezers or tip of scissors. With toes pointing forwards, sew cast-off stitches of legs to lower edge of body.

Short Sleeves, Arms and Hands
Sew up row ends of hands and place a small ball of stuffing into hands, pushing stuffing in with tweezers or tip of scissors. Sew up arms from wrists to underarm. Stuff arms, leaving armholes open. Sew arms to doll at either side, sewing cast-on stitches at top of arms to second row below neck.

Features
Start and finish off features at top of head under hair. Embroider eyes in black, marking their position on 6th row above neck with two clear knitted stitches in between. Work a vertical chain stitch for each eye, starting at marked position and finishing on row above. Embroider mouth in red on 2nd and 3rd below eyes making a shallow 'v' shape across two stitches. Shade cheeks with a red pencil.

Hair
Sew up row ends of hair and place on doll, pulling hair down to neck at back. Sew lower edge of hair to head all the way round.

Dungarees and Straps
Sew up leg seams of dungarees on right side from lower edge to crotch. Sew round crotch and sew up row ends at centre back. Place dungarees on doll and sew cast-off stitches at waist to first row of upper body. Sew ends of straps to bib, take straps over shoulders, cross them over and sew ends to waist of dungarees at back.

Pinafore and Straps
Sew up row ends of skirt of pinafore and place on doll. Sew cast-off stitches at waist to first row of upper body. Sew ends of straps to bib, take straps over shoulders, cross them over and sew ends to waist of pinafore at back.

Plaits or Bunches
Make plaits or bunches. For plaits, cut 6 lengths of yarn to match hair, each 15in (35cm) long and lay them in a bundle. Tie a knot at centre of bundle and fold in half. Divide into three and plait for 1in (2.5cm) and tie a knot. Trim ends beyond knot to ⅓in (1cm) and sew plaits to side of head. For bunches, take yarn to match hair and cut 25 strands, each 6in (15cm) approx and lay them in a bundle. Tie bundle in middle and fold in half. Cut ends to 1½in (4cm) from folded end. Repeat for second bunch and sew bunches to hair at sides. If yarn used is suitable, unravel strands for a 'frizzy' look.

Why is Mary so contrary?

SHOULD HUMPTY WEAR A CRASH HELMET?

Shall we buy the five monkeys a trampoline?

Where do cats go to learn the fiddle?

Techniques

Getting started

Buying yarn

All the patterns in this book are worked in double knitting yarn (DK yarn; known as light worsted in the US). There are many DK yarns on the market, from natural fibres to acrylic blends. Acrylic is a good choice, as it washes without shrinking, although you should always follow the care instructions on the ball band. Be cautious about using a brushed or mohair-type yarn if the toy is intended for a baby or a very young child, as the fluffy fibres could be swallowed.

Tension

Tension is not critical when knitting toys if the correct yarn and needles are used. All the toys in this book are knitted on 3.25mm (UK10:US3) knitting needles. This should turn out at approximately 26 stitches and 34 rows over 4in (10cm) square.

Slip knot

1 Leave a long length of yarn: as a rough guide, allow ⅜in (1cm) for each stitch to be cast on, plus an extra length for sewing up. Wind the yarn from the ball round your left index finger from front to back and then to front again. Slide the loop from your finger and pull the new loop through from the centre. Place this loop from back to front on to the needle that is in your right hand.

2 Pull the tail of yarn down to tighten the knot slightly and pull the yarn from the ball to form a loose knot.

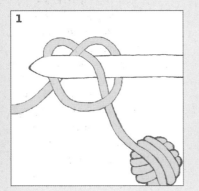

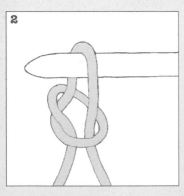

Casting on

Thumb method

1 Make a slip knot. Hold the needle in your right hand with your index finger on the slip knot loop to keep it in place.

2 Wrap the loose tail end round your left thumb, from front to back. Push the needle's point through the thumb loop from front to back. Wind the ball end of the yarn round the needle from left to right.

3 Pull the loop through the thumb loop, then remove your thumb. Gently pull the new loop tight using the tail yarn

Repeat this process until the required number of stitches are on the needle.

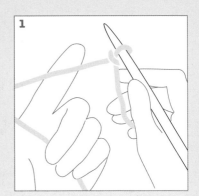

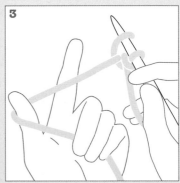

Knit stitch

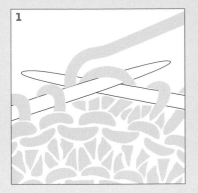

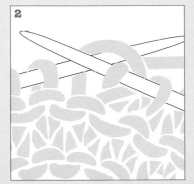

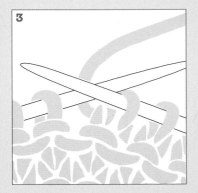

1 Hold needle with stitches in left hand. Hold yarn at back of work and insert point of right-hand empty needle into the front loop of the first stitch. Wrap yarn around point of right-hand needle in a clockwise direction using your index finger. Bring yarn through to front of work.

2 With yarn still wrapped around the point, bring the right-hand needle back towards you through the loop of the first stitch. Try to keep the free yarn fairly taut but not too slack or tight.

3 With the new stitch firmly on the right-hand needle, gently pull the old stitch to the right and off the tip of the left-hand needle. Repeat for all the knit stitches across the row.

Purl stitch

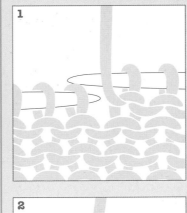

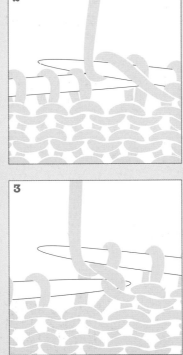

1 Hold needles with stitches in left hand and hold yarn at front of work.

2 Insert point of right-hand empty needle into the front loop of the first stitch. Wrap yarn around point of right-hand needle in an anti-clockwise direction using index finger. Bring yarn back to front of work.

3 With yarn still wrapped around point of right-hand needle, bring it back through the stitch. Try to keep free yarn taut but not too slack or tight. With the new stitch firmly on the right-hand needle, gently pull the old stitch off the tip of the left-hand needle. Repeat for all the purl stitches along the row.

techniques

Types of stitch

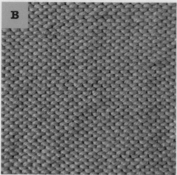

Moss stitch (D)

This stitch creates a bumpy-looking fabric made by alternating purl and knit stitches in a row. To create moss stitch, you need an odd number of stitches on the needle.

1 With the yarn at the back of the work, knit the first stitch in the normal way.

2 Bring the yarn through the two needles to the front of your work.

3 With the yarn now at the front, purl the stitch.

4 Next you need to knit a stitch, so take the yarn back between the needles and knit a stitch. Continue to k1, (p1, k1) to the end of the row. This row is repeated.

Garter stitch (A)

This is made by knitting every row.

Stocking stitch (B)

Probably the most commonly used stitch in knitting, this is created by knitting on the right side and purling on the wrong side.

Reverse stocking stitch (C)

This is made by purling on the right side and knitting on the wrong side.

Increasing

Three methods are used in this book for increasing the number of stitches: m1, kfb and pfb.

M1 Make a stitch by picking up the horizontal loop between the needles from front to back and placing it onto the left-hand needle. Now knit into the back of it to twist it, or purl into the back of it on a purl row.

Kfb Make a stitch on a knit row by knitting into the front then back of the next stitch. To do this, simply knit into the next stitch but do not slip it off. Take the point of the right-hand needle around and knit again into the back of the stitch before removing the loop from the left-hand needle. You now have made two stitches out of one.

Pfb Make a stitch on a purl row by purling into the front then back of the next stitch. To do this, purl the next stitch but do not slip it off the needle. Take the point of the right-hand needle around and purl again into the back of the stitch before removing the loop from the left-hand needle. You now have made two stitches out of one.

Decreasing

To decrease a stitch, simply knit two stitches together to make one stitch out of the two stitches, or if the instructions say k3tog, then knit three stitches together to make one out of the three stitches. To achieve a neat appearance to your finished work, this is done as follows:

At the beginning of a knit row and throughout the row, k2tog by knitting two stitches together through the front of the loops.

At the end of a knit row, if these are the very last two stitches in the row, then knit together through the back of the loops.

At the beginning of a purl row, if these are the very first stitches in the row, then purl together through the back of the loops. Purl two together along the rest of the row through the front of the loops.

Casting off

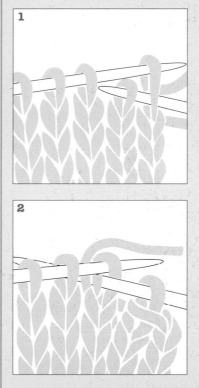

1 Knit two stitches onto the right-hand needle, then slip the first stitch over the second and let it drop off the needle. One stitch remains.

2 Knit another stitch so you have two stitches on the right-hand needle again.

Repeat the process until only one stitch is left on the left-hand needle. Break the yarn and thread it through the remaining stitch.

Threading yarn through stitches

Sometimes you will see 'thread yarn through stitches on needle, pull tight and secure'. To do this, first break the yarn, leaving a long end, and thread a needle with this end.

Pass the needle through all the stitches on the knitting needle, slipping each stitch off the knitting needle in turn. Draw the yarn through the stitches.

To secure, pass the needle once again through all the stitches in a complete circle and pull tight.

Placing a marker

When placing a marker on the cast-on edge, thread a needle with yarn in a contrasting colour and count the number of stitches to where the marker is to be

placed. Pass the needle between these stitches, tie a loose loop around the cast-on edge with a double knot and trim the ends. To place a marker on

a stitch, thread a needle with contrast yarn and pass this needle through the stitch on the knitting needle to be marked. Tie a loose loop with a double knot and trim the ends.

Sewing up

The characters in this book are put together using simple sewing techniques.

Sew up row ends
Pieces can be joined by oversewing on the wrong side and turning the piece the right side out. For smaller pieces, or pieces that cannot be turned, oversew on the right side.

Sew up striped row ends
Sew up row ends by sewing back and forth one stitch in from the edge on the wrong side.

Mattress stitch
Join row ends by taking small straight stitches back and forth on the right side of work (see illustration on left).

Running stitch
The necks of the dolls are shaped with a running stitch. Take a double length of yarn and thread a needle and take the needle in and out of every half stitch to create a line of gathering stitches around the neck. Do not secure either end of the yarn but pull both ends tight and knot yarn with a double knot. Then sew ends into neck.

Finishing touches

Embroidery

To begin embroidery invisibly, tie a knot in the end of the yarn. Take a large stitch through the work, coming up to begin the embroidery. Allow the knot to disappear through the knitting and be caught in the stuffing. To fasten off invisibly, sew a few stitches back and forth through the work, inserting the needle where the yarn comes out.

Long stitches

Embroider nostrils and some mouths by sewing long stitches.

Backstitch

Bring the needle out at the beginning of the stitch line, make a straight stitch and bring the needle out slightly further along the stitch line. Insert the needle at the end of the first stitch and bring it out still further along the stitch line. Continue in the same way to create a line of joined stitches.

Chain stitch

Bring the needle up through your work to start the first stitch and hold down the thread with the left thumb. Insert the needle in the same place and bring the point out a short distance away. Keeping the working thread under the needle point, pull the loop of thread to form a chain.

Making a twisted cord

A twisted cord is used for the mouse and cow's tail, the hanging cords for the spider and the cow jumping over the moon, and the strap for Boy Blue's horn.

1 Cut even strands of yarn to the number and length stated in the pattern and knot each end. Anchor one end – you could tie it to a door handle or a chair, or ask a friend to hold it.

2 Take the other end and twist until it is tightly wound.

3 Hold the centre of the cord, and place the two ends together. Release the centre, so the two halves twist together. Smooth it out and knot the ends together.

Stuffing and aftercare

Spend a little time stuffing your knitted figure evenly. Acrylic toy stuffing is ideal; use plenty, but not so much that it stretches the knitted fabric so the stuffing can be seen through the stitches. Fill out any base, keeping it flat so the figure will be able to stand upright. Tweezers are useful for stuffing small parts.

Washable filling is recommended for all the stuffed figures so that you can hand-wash them with a non-biological detergent. Do not spin or tumble dry, but gently squeeze the excess water out, arrange the figure into its original shape, and leave it to dry.

techniques

139

Abbreviations

alt	alternate
beg	beginning
cont	continue
dec	decrease/decreasing
DK	double knitting
foll	following
garter st	garter stitch: knit every row
inc	increase/increasing
k	knit
k2tog	knit two stitches together: if these are the very last in the row, then work together through back of loops
k3tog	knit three stitches together
kfb	make two stitches out of one: knit into the front then the back of the next stitch
k-wise	knit ways
LH	left hand
m1	make one stitch: pick up horizontal loop between the needles from front to back and work into the back of it to twist it
moss st	moss stitch: knit 1 stitch, (purl next stitch, knit next stitch) to end
patt	pattern
p	purl
p2tog	purl two stitches together: if these stitches are the very first in the row, then work together through back of loops
p3tog	purl three stitches together
pfb	make two stitches out of one: purl into the front then the back of the next stitch

p-wise	purl ways
rem	remaining
rep	repeat(ed)
rev st st	reverse stocking stitch: purl on the right side, knit on the wrong side
RH	right hand
RS	right side
slk	slip one stitch knit ways
slp	slip one stitch purl ways
st(s)	stitch(es)
st st	stocking stitch: knit on the right side, purl on the wrong side
tbl	through back of loop(s)
tog	together
WS	wrong side
yf	yarn forward
yb	yarn back
( )	repeat instructions between brackets as many times as instructed
*	repeat from * as instructed

Conversions

Knitting needles

UK:	US:	Metric:
8	6	4mm
10	3	3.25mm

Yarn weight

UK:	US:
Double knitting	Light worsted

Terms

UK:	US:
Cast off	Bind off
Moss stitch	Seed stitch
Stocking stitch	Stockinette stitch
Tension	Gauge
Yarn forward	Yarn over

Supplier

Sirdar Bonus DK
www.sirdar.co.uk
+44 (0)1924 371 501

About the author

Sarah Keen is passionate about knitting, finding it relaxing and therapeutic. She discovered her love of the craft at a very early age; her mother taught her to knit when she was just four years old and by the age of nine she was making jackets and jumpers.

Sarah now works as a freelance pattern designer and finds calculating rows and stitches challenging but fascinating. She is experienced in designing knitted toys for children, and also enjoys writing patterns for charity. This is her fourth book for GMC Publications; she is also the author of *Knitted Wild Animals*, *Knitted Farm Animals* and *Knitted Noah's Ark*.

Acknowledgements

Special thanks to Bethan – together we researched the book.

And many, many thanks to all supporting family and friends who enthused and enquired about this book at all stages of its coming together.

Also thanks to Cynthia (www.clarewools.co.uk) and to all the team at GMC.

Index

index

To place an order, or to request a catalogue, contact:
GMC Publications Ltd
Castle Place, 166 High Street, Lewes, East Sussex, BN7 1XU
United Kingdom
Tel: +44 (0)1273 488005
www.gmcbooks.com